EDEXCEL FOR GCSE THIF

PE

Sue Hartigan

DYNAMIC LEARNING

HODDER
EDUCATION
AN HACHETTE UK COMPANY

The Publishers would like to thank the following for permission to reproduce copyright material.

Acknowledgements

Every effort has been made to trace all copyright holders, but if any have been inadvertently overlooked, the Publishers will be pleased to make the necessary arrangements at the first opportunity.

Although every effort has been made to ensure that website addresses are correct at time of going to press, Hodder Education cannot be held responsible for the content of any website mentioned in this book. It is sometimes possible to find a relocated web page by typing in the address of the home page for a website in the URL window of your browser.

Hachette UK's policy is to use papers that are natural, renewable and recyclable products and made from wood grown in sustainable forests. The logging and manufacturing processes are expected to conform to the environmental regulations of the country of origin.

Orders: please contact Bookpoint Ltd, 130 Park Drive, Milton Park, Abingdon, Oxon OX14 4SE. Telephone: (44) 01235 827720. Fax: (44) 01235 400454. Email education@bookpoint.co.uk Lines are open from 9 a.m. to 5 p.m., Monday to Saturday, with a 24-hour message answering service. You can also order through our website: www.hoddereducation.co.uk

ISBN: 9781471866968

The writing of this book was completed in October 2015.

© Sue Hartigan 2016

First published in 2016 by

Hodder Education,

An Hachette UK Company

Carmelite House

50 Victoria Embankment

London EC4Y 0DZ

www.hoddereducation.co.uk

Impression number   10 9 8 7 6 5 4 3 2 1

Year   2019 2018 2017 2016

Cover photo Skynesher/Getty Images

Illustrations by Aptara

Typeset in India by Aptara Inc.

Printed in Italy

A catalogue record for this title is available from the British Library.

Contents

Chapter 1 The skeletal system and physical activity

Learning goals

By the end of this chapter you should be able to:

- apply the functions of the skeleton to performance in physical activity and sport
- identify the bones in the skeleton
- classify the bones of the skeleton, linking their classification to their function and use in physical activity and sport
- classify the joints of the skeleton and their impact on the range of movement
- explain the role of ligaments and tendons in physical activity and sport.

The functions of the skeleton

What does the skeleton do? The skeleton:

- **protects the body's vital organs.** The role of the skeleton to protect vital organs is very important in sport. For example, the ribs and sternum protect the heart and lungs if a batsman is struck with a cricket ball, the cranium protects the brain from head injury in rugby during tackles or racket injury in squash (if the opposition has a wide swing) and the pelvic girdle protects the intestines if there is a misplaced punch in boxing.

- **allows movement through the use of joints and muscle attachment.** Most sports involve a lot of movement, for example squash, football and netball would be impossible to play if we were unable to use any of our muscles to move our bones. We will see in the next chapter that the muscles pull on the bones to which they are attached to move them, for example, one end of the biceps muscle is attached to the lower arm, so as the muscle contracts, it pulls on the bone in the lower arm to bend the arm. We can only bend the arm, of course, as there is a joint between the lower and upper arm – the elbow.

- **helps formation of blood cells.** Platelets, red blood cells and most white blood cells are produced in the bone marrow. Platelets are critical to stopping bleeding if a performer receives a cut or a scratch during their activity. As they come into contact with the site of the tear, they stick to each other to block the tear in the wall of the blood vessel. Red blood cells transport oxygen and then exchange it for carbon dioxide. Red blood cells carry the oxygen that the performer needs to work aerobically. White blood cells are essential to help prevent infection, to keep the performer healthy.

- **stores minerals.** Bones store calcium and phosphorus. These minerals are needed to keep the bones healthy, reducing the risk of osteoporosis. If a sports performer did not have strong bones they would not be able to subject their bodies to the forces required in sport, for example, being thrown in a judo throw, falling from a horse or being accidentally hit in the shin by a hockey stick or ball.

Key words

Platelets – blood cells that clot together to heal a wound in the skin

Osteoporosis – health condition where the bones of the skeleton become brittle and more likely to break

Check your understanding

1. Why do we need red blood cells?

The bones of the skeleton

Figure 1.1 shows the major bones of the skeleton.

Actions

Once you have become familiar with the names of these bones, copy each of their names onto sticky labels and place them on a friend to help reinforce your understanding of the correct location of each bone.

There are two common errors or difficulties in learning the names of the bones of the skeleton.

1. Sometimes it is difficult to remember which of the bones is which in the lower leg. If you are having difficulty with this, it might be helpful to remember that the tibia is the thicker of the two bones and that the fibula is the finer (or 'f'inner!') of the two bones. It is also worth pointing out that you must make sure you do not confuse the endings of the names of these bones.

Check your understanding

2. State three functions of the skeleton.

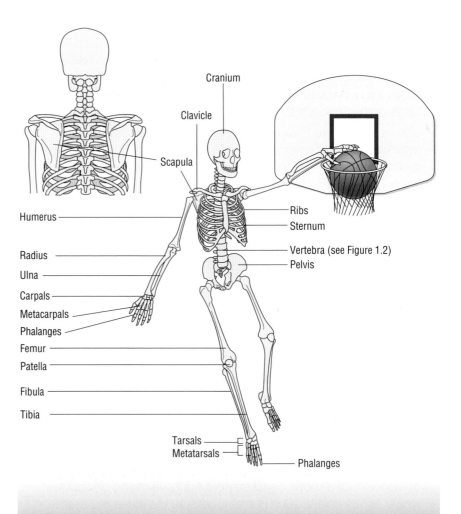

Figure 1.1 The human skeleton

2. A similar problem occurs with remembering the bones of the lower arm. In this case, try to remember that the radius is the right bone for the thumb; provided the diagram you are asked to label has the hand on it as well, this should not be a problem!

Classification and function of bones

All of the bones of the human skeleton can be classified according to their function. Bones are either:

- long
- short
- flat
- irregular.

Long bones

Bones are called long bones if they are longer in length than they are wide. These bones act as levers in the body, allowing us to move (with the help of muscles and joints).

Short bones

These are box-shaped, in that they tend to be as long as they are wide. Do any of the bones in Figure 1.1 fit this description? These bones are specially designed for strength or weight bearing and absorbing shock (for example running, handstands and other inverted balances or movements in gymnastics).

Flat bones

These bones are normally flat, thin and curved. Can you see any of these in Figure 1.1? These bones give protection and a large surface area for muscle attachment.

Irregular bones

Irregular bones are also used for protection and muscle attachment.

Look back at Figure 1.1. Are there any bones that you haven't been able to classify yet? Could these be irregular bones? If the shape of the bone doesn't fit any of the other descriptions, then it probably is irregular.

Actions

Copy and complete Table 1.1. Use Figure 1.1 to help you classify each of the labelled bones of the skeleton.

The bones of the vertebral column

This is made up of five regions. The bones in each of the regions are of different sizes and shapes and are all irregular bones. For example, the bones start off relatively small at the neck and increase in size as they need to support more of the body weight. Although the atlas and axis of the cervical region allow specific movements, the remaining vertebrae of the cervical, thoracic and lumbar regions all contribute to

Check your understanding

3. Identify the correct name for the 'shoulder blade'.

4. What is the function of a long bone?

Key words

Vertebral column – forms the spine in the body. It is made up of a number of vertebrae

Vertebrae – bones that form the spine or vertebral column

Atlas and axis – the two vertebrae at the top of the vertebral column that connect the vertebral column to the cranium

Cranium – anatomical name for the skull

BONES OF THE SKELETON	CLASSIFICATION OF BONE	ROLE IN PHYSICAL ACTIVITY
Cranium		
Clavicle		
Scapula		
Vertebral column		
Ribs		
Sternum		
Humerus		
Radius		
Ulna		
Carpals		
Metacarpals		
Phalanges		
Pelvis		
Femur		
Patella		
Tibia		
Fibula		
Tarsals		
Metatarsals		

Table 1.1 Classification of bones

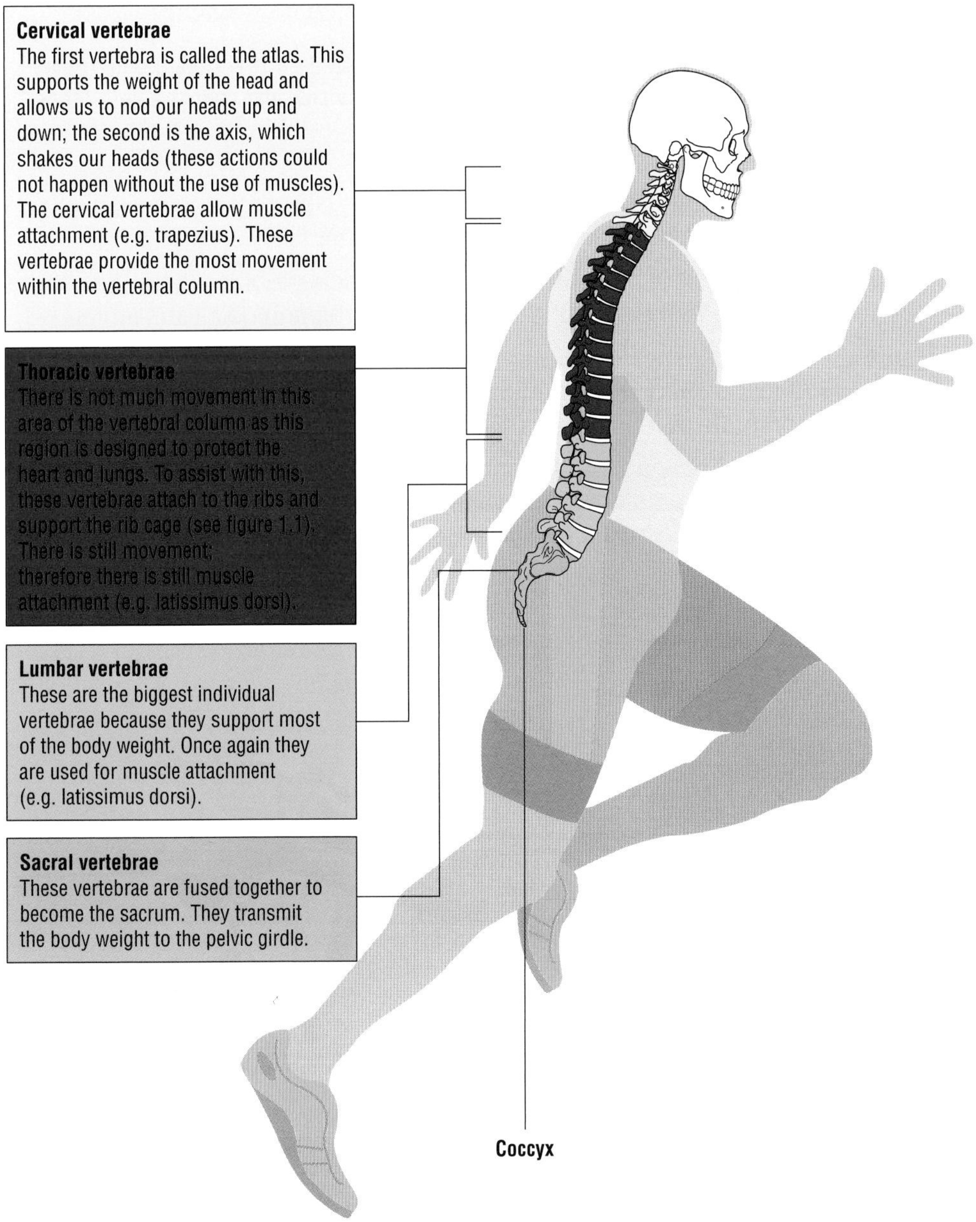

Cervical vertebrae
The first vertebra is called the atlas. This supports the weight of the head and allows us to nod our heads up and down; the second is the axis, which shakes our heads (these actions could not happen without the use of muscles). The cervical vertebrae allow muscle attachment (e.g. trapezius). These vertebrae provide the most movement within the vertebral column.

Thoracic vertebrae
There is not much movement in this area of the vertebral column as this region is designed to protect the heart and lungs. To assist with this, these vertebrae attach to the ribs and support the rib cage (see figure 1.1). There is still movement; therefore there is still muscle attachment (e.g. latissimus dorsi).

Lumbar vertebrae
These are the biggest individual vertebrae because they support most of the body weight. Once again they are used for muscle attachment (e.g. latissimus dorsi).

Sacral vertebrae
These vertebrae are fused together to become the sacrum. They transmit the body weight to the pelvic girdle.

Coccyx

Figure 1.2 The vertebral column

the movements possible at the spine, as they are jointed (see Figure 1.2). These movements are:

- flexion (bending forward)
- extension (bending backwards)
- lateral flexion (bending sideways)
- rotation (twisting and turning).

Discs of cartilage 'sit' between the vertebrae that move (Figure 1.3).

Use of the vertebral column in sport

The structure of the vertebral column makes it ideal to carry out its functions, all of which allow us to participate in sport.

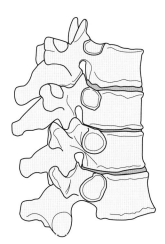

Figure 1.3 Vertebral discs

Actions

Look at the images in Figure 1.4. Discuss with a partner how the vertebral column assists these performers in their activities and compare your ideas with those shown.

- Movement of the head to aid technique (spotting landing, looking at track, tucking up in dive) by cervical vertebrae.
- Protection of heart and lungs by thoracic vertebrae when three of the four performers 'land' (the diver, high jump and pole vault athletes shown in Figure 1.4).
- Muscle attachment to allow the performers in Figure 1.4 to flex, extend or rotate as required by their technique.
- Weight bearing for the sprinter (and for the other three performers in Figure 1.4 leading up to their aspect of flight, for example, run up for pole vault) by the sacral vertebrae.

Figure 1.4

NAME OF JOINT	BONES THAT MAKE UP THE JOINT
Neck	
Elbow	
Knee	
Ankle	
Hip	
Shoulder	
Wrist	

Table 1.2 Bones that form a joint

Actions

Copy Table 1.2 and complete the second column using Figure 1.1.

Classification of joints

Joints are responsible for 'fitting' the skeleton together, along with ligaments. A need for strength makes the bones rigid, but if the skeleton consisted of one solid bone, movement would be nearly impossible (try running without bending your legs, or throwing a ball without bending your arm), therefore we have joints. A joint is a place where two or more bones meet.

The bones you should have identified when completing Table 1.2 will all form joints. You need to know the joints listed in Table 1.2 and you need to be able to classify these joints and know the range of movement possible at each one.

You need to be able to classify the joints listed in Table 1.2 as either:

- pivot (atlas and axis)
- hinge (elbow, knee, ankle)
- ball and socket (hip and shoulder)
- condyloid (wrist)

(There are other joint types, but these are not currently part of your course.)

Joints are classified into certain types depending on the amount of movement that can be carried out at them. For example, the movement possible at your knee is different from the movement possible at the shoulder.

The shoulder joint is the most freely moveable in the body. This obviously presents an advantage in terms of sport – look at the arm action in the butterfly stroke for swimming, or the bowling action in cricket, both demand a high level of flexibility. You cannot achieve this amount of movement at any other joint in the body. The disadvantage is that it is a relatively unstable joint and can dislocate.

The knee joint is most likely to cause problems in later life due to overuse in sport. It is put under a great deal of pressure from pounding when running and turning and from the knocks it receives in contact sports. Knee injuries are most common in sports that require twisting movements and sudden changes of direction, such as football, rugby, basketball, netball and skiing.

Movement at joints

The reason you need to know that there are different types of joints is that the type of joint will determine the type of movement we can do at that joint.

Key word

Dislocate – the separation of two (or more) bones where they meet at a joint

Study hints

Make sure you are familiar with the terminology that will be used in your exams. The knee is the name of the joint, but if asked to classify the knee joint you would need to know that it is a hinge joint.

Movements at joints are known as joint actions and are given specific names, as shown in Table 1.3.

JOINT ACTION	DESCRIPTION OF ACTION	EXAMPLE FROM SPORT	EXPLANATION
Flexion	Bending a limb at a joint		The elbow of the ball handler is bent
Extension	Straightening a limb at a joint		The arm holding the discus is straight
Abduction	Movement of a limb sideways away from the centre of the body		The gymnast's legs have been moved sideways away from the centre of the body
Adduction	Movement of a limb sideways towards the centre of the body		The gymnast's legs have moved together
Rotation Circumduction	Circular movement around the joint Conical movement allowing 360° rage of movement		The swimmer's arms make a circular action to complete the butterfly stroke
Dorsi-flexion	Bending of the foot at the ankle to pull the toes towards the shin		The long jumper is leading with their heels, trying to get them as far forward in the long jump pit as possible
Plantar-flexion	Bending of the foot at the ankle to point the toes away from the shin		The footballer is pointing their toes as they follow through from striking the ball

Table 1.3 Joint actions

NAME OF JOINT	BONES THAT MAKE UP THE JOINT	IMAGE OF THE JOINT
Elbow	Humerus, radius and ulna (Joint 1) and radius and ulna (Joint 32)	
Shoulder	Humerus Scapula	
Hip	Femur Hip (the fused bones of the ilium, ischium and pubis)	
Knee	Femur Tibia (Although the fibula is next to the tibia it is not involved in the movement at the joint. Similarly, the patella is there to protect the front of the joint)	
Neck	Atlas Axis (This is the name commonly given to this joint rather than neck)	

Table 1.4 Bones that form the joints

You can see examples of different joint actions every time you watch a sports performer. The athlete in Figure 1.5 is straightening his arm as he begins to pull the paddle back through the water. He is therefore extending (joint action) the arm at the elbow (joint).

In examination questions you will normally be expected to state the joint action as well as the type of movement. Remember that there should be two parts to your answer, the joint and the action occurring at it. You might even be asked to analyse a movement shown in a single image or as a movement changes from one image to the next. If you do, look at the image given and describe the movement you see, giving the joint action, the joint, and if the question asks for it, the muscles responsible for the movement (but more on that in the next chapter!).

Actions

Give examples of techniques from one of your practical activities (see activity list, p.216) that use each of the stated joint actions from Table 1.3.

Actions

Name the joints and the joint actions occurring at A and B in Figure 1.6A and Figure 1.6B on p.10.

Figure 1.5 Joint action in physical activity

Figure 1.6 A

Figure 1.6 B

Actions

Skill/technique	Joint	Joint action
Sprint start ('Set')	Knee	
	Hip	
	Elbow	
Stationary, inverted position in a handstand	Knee	
	Elbow	
Kicking the ball in football	Knee	
	Hip	
	Elbow	
Bowling the ball in cricket	Shoulder	
Completing a cartwheel	Elbow	
	Shoulder	

Table 1.5 Joint actions

Actions

Use a photo of yourself or a peer or role model performing in sport or taking part in a PE lesson. Place the photograph in the centre of a sheet of plain paper. Choose four of the seven joints you have to study and draw a small box around each one as shown in Figure 1.7. On your paper state the name and type of joint and the joint action that is happening in the image.

The elbow is a . . .

The knee is a . . .

Figure 1.7

The role of tendons and ligaments

Tendons: these attach muscles to bones. They are very tough as they have to withstand the force of the muscle contraction required to move the bone. They are also flexible so that they can cope with the flexion and extension of the muscle. If there is sudden exertion, tendons can snap or tear. If this is the Achilles tendon (at the heel) the performer will be out of action for weeks or even longer. Tendons can also become inflamed, making further use of the muscle painful. This condition is called tendonitis and is normally associated with overuse, for example, where a sports performer has increased their training intensity a bit too quickly.

Ligaments: these join bone to bone. They stabilise the joint by supporting it and limiting its movement, helping to prevent dislocation and movements that might result in breaks of the bone to which they are attached. They are slightly elastic and can stretch during a long exercise session, making the joint slightly less stable. However, once the performer has rested, the ligament will normally return to its original length. The ligaments in the ankle and knee often suffer sprains.

Check your understanding

5. Which classification of joint provides the greatest range of movement?

PRACTICE QUESTIONS

1. Explain why platelets are so important to performers in contact sports such as rugby.

2. Copy and complete the table about joints, joint classification and joint actions in physical activity.

Joint	Joint Classification	Joint action	Use in physical activity
Knee	Hinge		Creating more power as the ball is kicked
Ankle	Hinge	Plantar-flexion	
Shoulder		Circumduction	Bowling in cricket
Hip	Ball and socket		Pike jump in trampolining

3. Using an example, explain the role of short bones.

4. Analyse the joint actions of the athlete in Figure 1.5.

5. Explain why an increase in the strength of a ligament could be beneficial to a performer.

Summary

There are five functions of the skeleton that support our performance in physical activity and sport.

- The bones of the skeleton can be classified as long, short, flat or irregular.
- The bones of the skeleton form joints that allow a range of movement.
- Joints are classified by the movement possibilities at the joint.
- Ligaments stabilise the bones in the joints so they do not dislocate when we move.
- Tendons attach muscle to bone, so when the muscle contracts we can move.

Useful websites

Skeletal system: Facts, function and diseases
www.livescience.com/22537-skeletal-system.html

Infant skull and fontanelles
www.innerbody.com/image/skel01.html

Human anatomy – skeleton
www.bbc.co.uk/science/humanbody/body/factfiles/
skeleton_anatomy.shtml

Chapter 2 The muscular system and physical activity

Learning goals

By the end of this chapter you should be able to:

- classify muscles as voluntary, involuntary or cardiac and give examples of each type and their characteristics
- locate and describe the functions and actions of the main muscles responsible for sporting movement
- analyse the use of 'antagonistic pairs' of muscles to bring about movement in physical activity and sport
- classify muscle fibres as either slow twitch or fast twitch, and link them to specific sporting activities due to their characteristics.

All sports performers need to be able to move. Movement is possible through the use of muscles, but not all muscles bring about movement.

Classification of muscles

Muscles can be voluntary, involuntary or cardiac. All are essential, but each type fulfils a different role within the body.

Cardiac muscle

Cardiac muscle is only found in the heart and is a special form of involuntary muscle, in that we have no direct conscious control over it. It also differs from voluntary muscle in that it does not tire, but continues to contract and relax throughout our lives. When the heart's cardiac muscle contracts it squeezes the blood in the heart through and then out of the heart so blood can be circulated around the body. When our heart rate increases, the cardiac muscle contracts more often, increasing the speed that blood can leave the heart so that more blood can be circulated around the body per minute.

Involuntary muscle

Involuntary muscle is found in the walls of organs in the body; for example in the arteries where they control blood flow by altering the size of the lumen in the artery (see section on vascular shunting, p. 23). This is important to the performer as this will control oxygen delivery and removal of carbon dioxide.

Parts of the digestive tract have involuntary muscles, where the action of the muscle contracting squeezes food further along, so it can be digested and essential nutrients extracted for energy for the performer to use.

Involuntary muscles are also responsible for regulating the flow of air through the lungs. Involuntary muscles know when to contract because they react to what is happening within the body. This means that we do not have to consciously control them; as they work on their own as they need to ensure the body is functioning properly.

Key words

Voluntary muscle – muscle that is consciously controlled by the individual, for example the muscles of the skeletal system

Conscious control – we need to think about the movement we want the muscles to do in order to execute it; it will not happen automatically

Skeletal muscle – muscles attached to the skeleton that contract to bring about movement

Involuntary muscle – muscle that is not consciously controlled by the individual, for example, the muscles in the digestive system

Cardiac muscle – specialised muscle found in the heart

Lumen – the space inside a tube, for example, the space the blood flows through inside the blood vessel

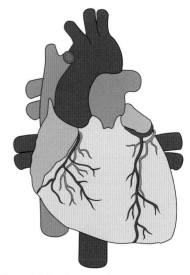

Figure 2.1 Cardiac muscle

Voluntary muscle

This is also referred to as skeletal muscle. It is the muscle type responsible for bringing about movement and maintaining body posture. We do think about using these muscles – they only move when we ask them to, in other words they are under our conscious control. See Figure 2.2 for the names of the muscles that you need to know for this course.

Functions of the voluntary muscular system and antagonistic muscle pairs

Figure 2.2 shows two volleyball players and a closer look at their muscular system.

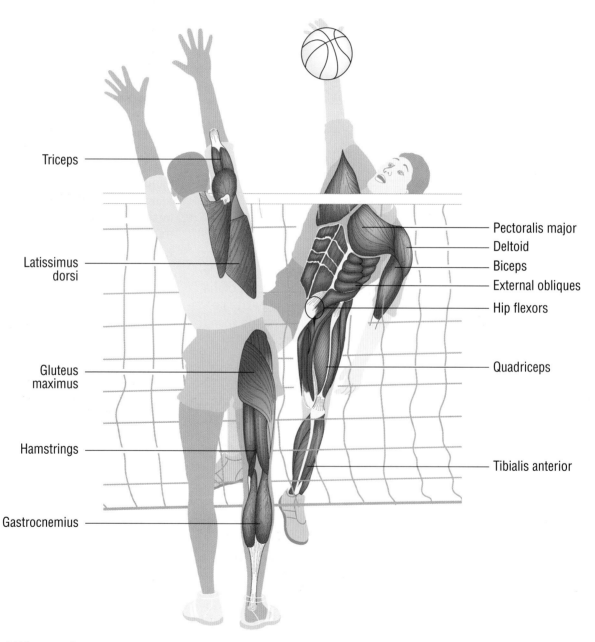

Figure 2.2 The muscular system

In order to bring about movement, our muscles contract – they can only pull, not push. They are attached to bones at both ends. One end is fixed and cannot move, so as the muscle contracts, the fixed end (the origin) pulls on the other end of the muscle, which is attached to a different bone. Because this end of the muscle can move (the insertion), it and the bone(s) it is attached to will be pulled towards the other end of the muscle and the bone it is attached to. Look at Figure 2.3 for an example. (Please note: you do not need to know about the origin and insertion of muscles for the exam, but it may help you to know, because then you can work out the action of the muscle.)

The biceps are attached to the scapula (origin) and the radius (insertion). Therefore the end of the muscle near the shoulder does not move, but the other end attached to the lower arm does move. When the muscle contracts, the end at the shoulder stays still, but the end attached to the lower arm moves and brings the bones of the lower arm with it – this is flexion at the elbow.

Having completed this movement, how do you move your arm back to its original position? A volleyball player smashing the ball will need flexion at the elbow, but then they will need to extend the arm at the elbow to get ready to dig, set or block the opponent's next shot. By relaxing the biceps and contracting the triceps, the triceps pull the lower arm back down to a straight position. Thus there is:

- flexion of the arm at the elbow caused by the biceps and
- extension of the arm at the elbow brought about by the triceps.

The biceps and triceps are working as an antagonistic pair: one muscle contracts (while the other relaxes the antagonist) to bring about a movement. You need to know several pairs of muscles that work in this way, as antagonistic pairs.

You should realise that muscle action is complicated, as many muscles often contribute to the action. For your course you should try to focus on the obvious movements that these 12 muscles bring about, this is summarised in Table 2.1.

Actions

Design a weight training session or a circuit that will exercise all of the muscles identified in Table 2.1. Copy Table 2.1 and add your stations or exercises to complete it.

Actions

Look at the images in Figure 2.4. Name two joints in each image and state the muscle action that has taken place at that joint and the muscles responsible for the movement.

Figure 2.4 The musculo-skeletal system in action

Key words

Origin and insertion – the points where a muscle attaches to a bone

Origin – the fixed end of the muscle attachment; when the muscle contracts this end of the bone will not move

Insertion – the end of the muscle that is attached to the bone that will move when the muscle contracts

Flexion – reducing the angle between bones at a joint, for example, when bending the arm at the elbow

Extension – increasing the angle between bones at a joint, for example, when straightening the arm at the elbow

Antagonistic muscle pairs – pairs of muscles that work together to bring about movement. In order to allow the agonist to contract, the antagonist muscle relaxes

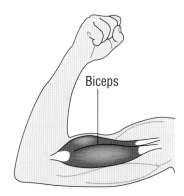

Figure 2.3 The biceps muscle contracts and pulls on the radius in the lower arm to bend the arm at the elbow.

MUSCLE	MUSCLE ACTION/ROLE	EXAMPLE USE	STATION TO EXERCISE THIS MUSCLE
Triceps	Extends lower arm at the elbow	Volleyball player has arms outstretched to block the ball	
Biceps	Flexes arm at the elbow	Tennis serve – racket preparation, when racket is behind head	
Deltoids	Abducts upper arm at the shoulder	Preparation for a cartwheel in gymnastics	
Pectorals	Adduction of upper arm at the shoulder	Arm action in front crawl (pull)	
Latissimus dorsi	Adducts and rotates the humerus at the shoulder (draws the arm back and in towards the body)	Pulling the arm back in archery	
External obliques	Laterally flex and rotate spine	Follow through at the hips after driving a golf ball	
Gluteus maximus	Extends the leg at the hip	Running action, one leg is left stretched back behind the other	
Hip flexors	Flexes the leg at the hip	Allows you to lift the knee when running	
Quadriceps	Extends the leg at the knee	Follow through after kicking a ball in football	
Hamstrings	Flexes the leg at the knee	Taking the leg back in preparation to strike the ball in a drop goal attempt in rugby	
Gastrocnemius	Plantar flexion of the foot	Going up onto toes prior to take off in a diving competition	
Tibialis anterior	Dorsi-flexion of the foot	Driving heel forward with toes up in leg shoot in long jump	

Table 2.1 Muscle action and movement in physical activity and sport

Check your understanding

3. Think about the location of the hamstrings. Which joint do they move? Will they flex or extend this joint?

Key words

Abduction – movement of the limb away from the body

Adduction – movement of the limb inwards and across the centre of the body

Lateral flexion – sideways bending movement

Actions

Look at the muscles and their actions in Table 2.1. Work out the antagonistic pairs of muscles in the table that bring about flexion and extension at a joint. Compare your answers with those shown in Table 2.2 at the end of the chapter.

Actions

Record one minute of practical performance of an activity of your choice. Analyse the movements that take place in that one minute and answer the following questions:

Give two different examples of techniques used in the video during the performance.

Analyse these techniques:
- State the action at the joints involved in the techniques.
- State the muscles responsible for bringing about the actions.
- State the antagonistic muscle that was relaxing to allow the movement to take place.
- State the type of joint where the action took place.
- Name the antagonistic muscle pairs that were used in the 1-minute video.

Characteristics of fast and slow twitch muscle fibre types

Muscle fibre types can be fast or slow twitch.

Skeletal muscle is made up of fast and slow twitch muscle fibres. The percentage of slow or fast twitch fibres that we have is inherited. Both fibre types have their advantages and disadvantages. A high percentage of fast twitch fibres would give us an advantage in anaerobic activities such as sprinting, whereas a high percentage of slow twitch muscle fibres would give us an advantage in endurance events.

Slow twitch fibres are also known as type I muscle fibres. They are efficient at using oxygen to release energy but are slower to contract than fast twitch fibres, type II, which means that they are not as powerful. They are good at using oxygen as they have:

- large amounts of myoglobin
- a large number of mitochondria
- a good capillary network.

These three things mean they are slow to fatigue, which is why they would be an advantage to an endurance athlete.

Fast twitch fibres can contract quickly, increasing the amount of force that can be exerted by the muscle over a short period of time. The disadvantage with these muscle fibre types is that they tire quickly. There are two types of fast twitch fibres:

- type IIa fibres are thought to be a 'hybrid' of type I and type IIx and they have some of the properties of each. With appropriate training it is thought that these muscle fibre types can be adapted to either be better for endurance or for power events by improving the relevant characteristics of the fibre type.

- type IIx fatigue easily as they do not have the myoglobin, mitochondria or large capillary network of slow twitch fibres. However, they can contract very quickly. This means they can generate more power than slow twitch fibres and type IIa, therefore they would be good for events requiring speed or large amounts of force.

Key words

Plantar flexion – extension of the ankle through pointing of the toes

Dorsi flexion – flexion of the foot in an upward direction by bringing toes up towards shin

Rotation – circular movement

Slow twitch or type I muscle fibres – good for endurance activities as they are slow to tire

Fast twitch or type II muscle fibres – can generate more force but tire more quickly, so are used in anaerobic work

Aerobic – with oxygen

Anaerobic – without oxygen

Check your understanding

4. Name the antagonistic muscle pair that allows movement of the ankle.

5. Which muscle fibre type can contract the most forcibly?

Actions

The characteristics of the fibre types make them suitable for different activities. Match the activities listed to the most appropriate muscle fibre type:

- sprint start
- sprint finish of 3000 metres
- middle of 3000 metres
- holding a handstand
- elite tennis player serving an ace in tennis
- footballer maintaining quality of play over length of match
- gymnast performing a tumbling routine as part of a floor routine

ANTAGONISTIC PAIR	JOINT	MUSCLE ACTION/ROLE
Triceps	Elbow	Extends lower arm at the elbow
Biceps		Flexes arm at the elbow
Gluteus maximus	Hip	Extends the leg at the hip
Hip flexors		Flexes the leg at the hip
Quadriceps	Knee	Extends the leg at the knee
Hamstrings		Flexes the leg at the knee
Gastrocnemius	Ankle	Plantar flexion of the foot
Tibialis anterior		Dorsi-flexion of the foot

Table 2.2 Antagonistic muscle pairs

Study hints

Don't be tempted to abbreviate technical terms. You need to demonstrate your knowledge in your exam, so use full muscle names to show you know them!

PRACTICE QUESTIONS

1. Explain how one characteristic of involuntary muscles makes them suitable for their role.

2. Read each statement and identify the muscle responsible for the stated action.
   (a) The _____ and _____ allows movement of the leg at the hip to improve their running technique.
   (b) The _____ allow the player to extend the leg at the knee after the shot.

3. Describe how antagonistic muscle action at the elbow is used in the racket arm during a tennis serve.

4. Explain why high numbers of capillaries in slow twitch muscle fibres is an advantage for endurance runners.

5. Explain why a long distance runner would also benefit from some type IIx muscle fibres.

Summary

- Muscles can be classified as voluntary, involuntary or cardiac.
- Each voluntary muscle has a specific function.
- Muscles are organised into antagonistic pairs to bring about movement.
- Muscles are made up of muscle fibres. These muscle fibres can be classified as type I, type IIa or type IIx.
- Each muscle fibre type is suited to a particular type of activity.

Useful websites

Muscular system
www.innerbody.com/image/musfov.html

Muscle types
www.training.seer.cancer.gov/anatomy/muscular/types.html

Major muscles – crossword

www.anatomyarcade.com/games/crosswords/majorMusclesC/majorMusclesCW.html

Chapter 3 The cardiovascular system and physical activity

Learning goals

By the end of this chapter you should be able to:

- apply the functions of the cardiovascular system to performance in physical activity
- identify the components of the heart and explain their role
- identify the differences between arteries, capillaries and veins and relate these differences to the importance of each vessel type during physical activity and sport
- describe vascular shunting and understand the reasons why it is necessary during physical activity
- explain the importance of the components of the blood for physical activity and sport.

This chapter looks at the cardiovascular system – the heart, blood and blood vessels. The cardiovascular system is vital for sporting performance as it is responsible for:

- transporting increased levels of oxygen (needed to release energy to perform and/or recover from performance) around the body to where it is needed
- regulating our temperature so that we do not overheat during exercise
- removing waste such as carbon dioxide and lactic acid
- transporting nutrients
- clotting of open wounds.

Although this chapter looks at the cardiovascular system, there are clear links with the respiratory system (see Chapter 4 on the respiratory system, p. 30) , as it is the respiratory system that is responsible for ensuring we get the required oxygen we need into our bodies. The two systems together are known as the cardio-respiratory system.

The Heart

The heart works continuously throughout our lives. In an average lifetime it can beat over three billion times. Try working it out: average heart rate (72 beats per minute (bpm)) X number of minutes in a day X number of days in a year X average life expectancy (80). This is a resting value for the heart rate; if we exercise, it beats even more.

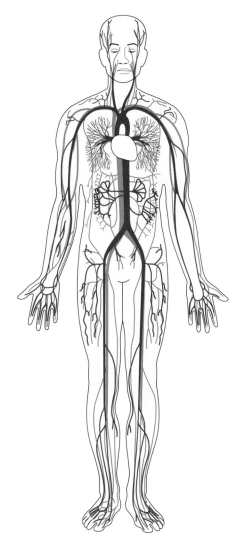

Figure 3.1 The cardiovascular system

Actions

There are ten components of the heart that you need to know:

atria, ventricles, septum, tricuspid valve, bicuspid valve, semi-lunar valves, aorta, vena cava, pulmonary artery, pulmonary vein.

Copy Figure 3.2 and label the diagram using the description of the heart and its components.

Key word

Atria – the plural of atrium, the upper chambers of the heart

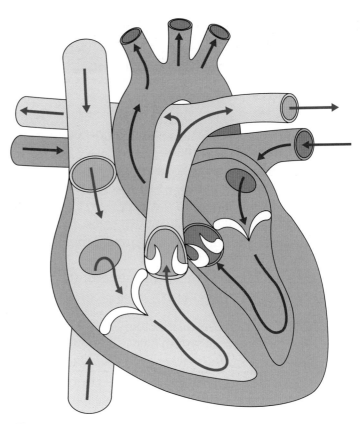

Figure 3.2 The heart

The heart is made up of four chambers. The top two chambers are called atria and the bottom chambers are the ventricles. They are assigned a side, left or right. This is the first tricky bit. When labelling the heart you have to imagine that it is in your body when deciding which is left and right. Which is the right side of your body? If you were to look at a photograph of the side you have just identified, your right would appear to be your left! If you pick up the photograph and turn it to face the same way that you are facing, your right side is back where it belongs, on the right of your body. The same is true with the heart, so when you look at a diagram, do not forget to imagine it inside your body.

The left and right atria receive blood into the heart and pass it on to the ventricles when they contract.

The left atrium receives oxygenated blood from the lungs through the pulmonary vein and the right atrium receives deoxygenated blood from the body through the vena cava (this is also a vein). Notice that atria is the plural form of atrium. You use it when talking about both atria rather than just one atrium.

Oxygenated means that the red blood cells have collected oxygen from the lungs (more on that in the next Chapter, see p. 33). Deoxygenated means that the oxygen that was being carried by the blood has been removed or taken by the body's tissues to use to release energy.

The left and right ventricles receive blood from the atria above them; once they have received the blood they contract to force the blood out of the heart.

Key words

Deoxygenated blood – blood that is returning to the lungs to pick up fresh oxygen

Oxygenated blood – blood that is travelling to the body carrying oxygen for use by the muscles

The left ventricle has a thicker muscular wall because it has to do the most work; it is from here that blood is pumped out of the heart via the aorta to the rest of the body. The aorta is an artery.

The right ventricle only pumps blood as far as the lungs, via the pulmonary artery to pick up more oxygen.

Three of the remaining four words that you need to know are all valves. Valves are flaps, which only allow blood to flow one way, like emergency exit doors that hinge one way to let you out, but close after you so that you cannot go back the way you came.

If blood were allowed to flow backwards, it might not be pushed to the lungs to collect extra oxygen or be pumped around the body to the tissues that need to receive oxygenated blood. In other words, we would be unlikely to receive the oxygen we needed to complete exercise.

The **tricuspid valve** is on the right side of the heart (one way to remember this is to think of a saying like 'it's all right to watch TV': TV stands for tricuspid valve, and it is on the right). The tricuspid valve separates the right atrium from the right ventricle, allowing blood to flow from the atrium to the ventricle.

The **bicuspid valve** is on the left side of the heart separating the left atrium from the left ventricle. It allows blood to flow from the left atrium to the left ventricle, but not the other way.

The remaining valves, between the left ventricle and the aorta and the right ventricle and the pulmonary artery, are called the **semi-lunar valves**. These valves allow the movement of blood from the ventricles out of the heart, but once it has left, the blood is not allowed to return.

The final label is the **septum**. This is the wall between the two sides of the heart, dividing left and right. This wall is required because the right side of the heart contains blood from the body that has been deoxygenated, whereas the blood on the left side of the heart contains oxygenated blood. If the blood were allowed to mix, the performer would receive a drop in the amount of oxygen being delivered to the muscles, so they would be unable to release as much energy for physical work.

You should now be able to finish labelling your diagram. Compare your answers with those shown in Figure 3.5.

Double circulatory system

As the heart pumps, it circulates blood. Blood is circulated from the heart to the lungs and then back to the heart (circuit 1, the pulmonary circulation). Blood is also circulated from the heart to the rest of the body and back again (circuit 2, the systemic circulation). Because of these two clear areas that are circulated (lungs and the rest of the body), it is known as a double circulatory system.

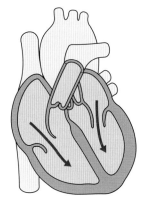

Figure 3.3 Ventricles fill with blood due to the contraction of the atria

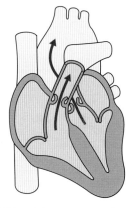

Figure 3.4 Ventricles contract to force blood out of the heart

Check your understanding

1. Identify the type or classification of heart muscle.

2. Name the chamber of the heart that supplies blood to the aorta.

3. Why is it important that blood circulates the lungs?

4. Why can't the blood just go straight to the body from the lungs. Why does it need to go back to the heart first?

Actions

Starting with blood entering the heart from the body, take it in turns in your class to state the next stage of the circulation. You should say whether blood is entering or leaving and which vessel or chamber it enters or leaves through, as well as the valves involved, until you have completed the route of the blood in the double circulation.

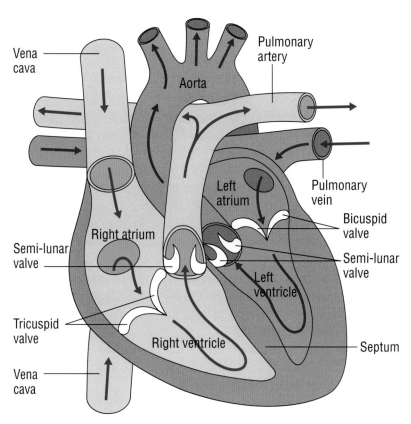

Figure 3.5 The heart (labelled)

Key words

Blood pressure – pressure exerted by the blood on the walls of the blood vessel

Systolic blood pressure – blood pressure when the heart is contracting

Diastolic blood pressure – blood pressure exerted on the walls of the arteries when the heart is resting, for example, between heartbeats

Check your understanding

5. Which type of blood vessel contains arterial blood?

Blood Pressure

As the blood moves through the blood vessels it exerts a force on the sides of the blood vessel it is travelling through. The strength of this force is your blood pressure. As the blood circulates further from the heart the force it exerts reduces, so blood pressure decreases as the blood moves through the arteries, into the capillaries and then on to the veins. When blood pressure is measured (as part of a health check) arterial blood pressure is used.

Blood pressure is checked because if your blood pressure is too high, it puts extra strain on your arteries (and your heart), which may lead to heart attacks and strokes.

When the ventricles contract, blood pressure is at its greatest. This is called systolic blood pressure. When the ventricles are filling, the blood pressure is lower (you would expect this, as blood is not being forced out of the heart). This is the diastolic blood pressure.

When your blood pressure is measured it will be written as two numbers. For example, if your reading is 120/80 mmHg, your systolic blood pressure is 120 mmHg and your diastolic blood pressure is 80 mmHg. mmHg is the unit used to give a value to pressure, in this case it is the unit of measurement for blood pressure, it stands for 'millimetre of mercury'.

Heart rate

Heart rate refers to the number of times the heart beats per minute. Each time the heart beats, the ventricles contract, squeezing blood out of the heart into the lungs or the rest of the body. During exercise we need to increase the rate of blood flow. In other words, we need to make the blood flow faster so that we can deliver oxygen more quickly to the working muscles and remove waste products, such as carbon dioxide, at a quicker rate. This means the performer can keep working at a higher level of intensity than when they are at rest. This increase in blood flow is mainly achieved through increasing the heart rate.

Stroke volume

This is the amount of blood ejected from the heart per beat. When the ventricles contract, they do not empty completely of blood: only about 60 per cent of the blood is ejected. With exercise, the muscles of the wall of the heart surrounding the ventricles become stronger so that when they contract they can do so more forcibly. When this happens, they can squeeze harder on the blood in the ventricles and therefore push more out of the heart. This is why stroke volume increases with regular exercise. Think of a balloon filled with water: if you squeeze it a little bit, a small amount of water comes out, but if you squeeze it harder, more water will be ejected.

The increase in stroke volume that is achieved through training also explains why fit performers tend to have lower resting heart rates than those who do not train.

Cardiac output

This is the amount of blood ejected from the heart per minute. It is calculated by multiplying heart rate (the number of times the heart beats per minute) by stroke volume (the amount of blood that is ejected from the heart per beat).

cardiac output = stroke volume X heart rate

At rest we need about 5 litres of blood to circulate our bodies per minute, but this figure can rise dramatically during exercise to 30 litres of blood per minute to make sure we have the oxygen we need and are able to remove the increased levels of carbon dioxide from the muscles.

> **Actions**
>
> Calculate the resting cardiac output (L/min) for a performer who has a:
> - resting heart rate of 70bpm
> - resting stroke volume of 70ml

Vascular shunting

At rest there is enough blood circulating our bodies to carry out the functions the body needs, for example, nutrients can be digested and sufficient oxygen is available to provide the energy needed. But how we use the blood flow will vary, depending on the needs of the body. For example, if we have just eaten there will be an increased need for blood flow to the digestive system. Therefore, a large percentage of the blood circulating the body is directed to the liver and kidneys so that digestive

> **Actions**
>
> Working in pairs, measure each other's resting heart rate and make a note of it. Find your pulse by placing two fingers on the inside of the wrist of your other hand, the same side as the thumb, and then count the number of times you feel the blood pulsate under your fingers in a minute, or 15 seconds, and multiply by 4. You need to stay calm and quiet while your pulse is being measured as any movement or sudden noise will make your heart beat faster.
>
> Take it in turns to carry out some exercise. This could be jumping up and down or running on the spot for two minutes. Immediately after your exercise, ask your partner to measure your heart rate again and make a note of it. Then swap roles.
>
> There should be a difference in your heart rate after exercise. Was it higher or lower? Why has your heart rate changed in this way?

> **Key words**
>
> **L/min** – unit of measurement to show the volume of fluid flowing in a minute. It is used here to represent cardiac output, for example, the number of litres of blood leaving the heart per minute
>
> **Vascular shunting** – increase in blood flow to active areas during exercise by diverting blood away from inactive areas
>
> **Vasoconstriction** – mechanism to reduce blood flow by reducing internal diameter of a blood vessel
>
> **Vasodilation** – mechanism to increase blood flow by widening the internal diameter of a blood vessel

functions can be carried out. Although blood is still flowing to all parts of the body, the amount available for the skeletal muscles (the muscles we use for physical activity) is reduced. This isn't a problem while at rest because there is still sufficient blood to transport the required oxygen to the muscles (the muscles use less oxygen when at rest than when exercising as they do not need as much energy).

A problem will arise if we need to exercise, because if blood flow remained the same there would not be enough oxygen delivered to the muscles. To overcome this problem, we can:

- increase cardiac output by increasing heart rate so that rather than circulating 5.5 litres of blood per minute we circulate 30 litres of blood per minute
- redistribute blood flow so that a greater percentage flows to the working muscles.

When we exercise, blood is redistributed so that a greater percentage of it (from 20 per cent to 80 per cent) flows to the skeletal muscles (this is so that it can provide oxygen and remove carbon dioxide so the muscles can continue to function when we ask them to work harder).

The process to allow us to redistribute blood in this way is called vascular shunting and is achieved through:

- vasodilation – is the relaxation of the muscular wall in the blood vessel (arteriole) causing the internal diameter of the blood vessel to become wider, so more blood can flow through. (The actual vessel doesn't become bigger, just the space within it that allows more blood to pass through.)
- vasoconstriction – this is the opposite to vasodilation. It means the muscular walls of the arteriole have contracted so that less blood can flow through the vessel.

Actions

Look at the two images of Dame Kelly Holmes: in Figure 3.6 she is resting after completing her race, and in Figure 3.7 she is in the middle of her event.

While she is running she will need to deliver more oxygen to her muscles than when she is at rest. She will also need to remove the increased carbon dioxide that is being created during exercise. Explain two ways her cardiovascular system will try to ensure she receives the oxygen she needs and is able to remove the additional carbon dioxide being created so she can continue with her winning performance.

Figure 3.6 Dame Kelly Holmes celebrating after her event

Figure 3.7 Dame Kelly Holmes in action

Actions

Look at the two images of the blood vessel in Figure 3.8.

1. Which blood vessel, A or B, is vasodilated?
2. Which blood vessel A or B, is vasoconstricted?
3. What would happen to the blood flow in vessel B compared with that in vessel A?
4. Which blood vessel, A or B, represents a blood vessel in skeletal muscle during exercise? Explain your answer.

Check your understanding

6. Do we need to consciously tell the blood vessel to increase or decrease its internal diameter? Therefore, what is the classification of this muscle type?

A    B

Figure 3.8 Blood flow

Blood vessels

Blood vessels carry blood to and from all the living cells in the body. There are different types of blood vessels: you need to know about arteries, capillaries and veins. Each type of blood vessel has a specific job to do and is structured differently so that it can do its job effectively.

Arteries

These carry blood away from the heart, which is easy to remember as away and arteries both start with the letter A. Also helping us is the fact that the aorta, the main artery, also starts with an A.

Arteries are made up of three layers: the outside layer is tough, the middle layer is muscular and the inner layer is smooth to make it easy for the blood to pass through.

Things to remember about arteries:

- They carry blood away from the heart.
- They carry blood at higher pressure than the other vessels because they take blood from the heart.
- They have thick muscular walls.
- They pulsate: when the heart relaxes, the artery muscle contracts, pushing the blood forward.
- Because they carry blood away from the heart they carry oxygenated blood. (There is ONE exception to this, can you work it out? Go back to Figure 3.5, remember arteries take blood away from the heart. Which of the blood vessels leaving the heart would have deoxygenated blood?)

Veins

Veins carry blood back to the heart. The main vein is called the vena cava.

Things to remember about veins:

- They carry blood towards the heart.
- They carry blood at low pressure.
- They have valves.
- They have thin walls.
- They have a larger internal lumen (the space in the middle of the vessel) than arteries.
- Because they carry blood back to the heart, they carry deoxygenated blood. (There is ONE exception to this, can you work it out? Go back to Figure 3.5, remember veins take blood back to the heart. Where would the blood vessel have needed to come from to have picked up oxygen? Which of the blood vessels taking blood to the heart would have oxygenated blood?)

Capillaries

If arteries take blood away from the heart and veins bring it back, how does the blood get from the artery into the vein? Via **capillaries**. These blood vessels form the link between the other two. This is where carbon dioxide will diffuse from the tissues into the blood and oxygen will diffuse from the blood to the tissues.

See Figure 3.10: the fine network of blood vessels between the larger two are the capillaries.

Things to remember about capillaries:

- They are the link between arteries and veins.
- They are one cell thick and very fragile.
- Blood cells pass through them one cell at a time (giving time for the exchange of gases to take place).

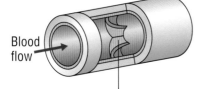

Figure 3.9 A vein

Figure 3.10 Capillaries between the larger blood vessels

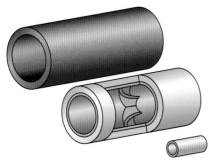

Figure 3.11 Three types of blood vessel

Actions

Look at Figure 3.11. Using your knowledge of the structure of the different types of blood vessels, identify each of the vessels in the image and justify your choice.

Actions

Use the descriptions of the blood vessels in this chapter to help you decide whether the following descriptions are of arteries, capillaries or veins:

1. I always travel away from the heart.
2. I am the link between the other two types of blood vessels.
3. I have thin walls.
4. I normally carry oxygenated blood.
5. I have thick muscular walls.
6. I have a small lumen (the lumen is the space in the middle of the vessel).
7. I allow the exchange of gases and nutrients with the cells of the body.
8. I always travel towards the heart.
9. I pulsate.
10. I work under high pressure.

The blood

Blood is made up of red blood cells, white blood cells, platelets and plasma. Adults have around 5.5 litres of blood circulating their bodies.

Plasma

This is the liquid part of the blood; it is mainly made up of water. If the plasma did not exist, the solid cells would not be able to flow around the body, so the plasma gives the other cells a ride.

Red blood cells

These are very important to a performer. The red blood cells contain haemoglobin, a substance that allows the transportation of oxygen around the body.

White blood cells

These are also very important to the performer. They are responsible for seeking out and destroying infections. The white cells can slide through the walls of the blood vessel and attack bacteria at the site of the infection. The white blood cells keep the performer healthy.

Platelets

These play a vital role in maintaining the health of a sports performer. Platelets aid clotting: if the performer receives a cut or a graze, platelets are dispatched to put a plug in the hole in the skin so that there is no further blood loss.

Check your understanding

7. Where are the blood cells made in the body?

Actions

Copy and complete the crossword on the cardiovascular system.

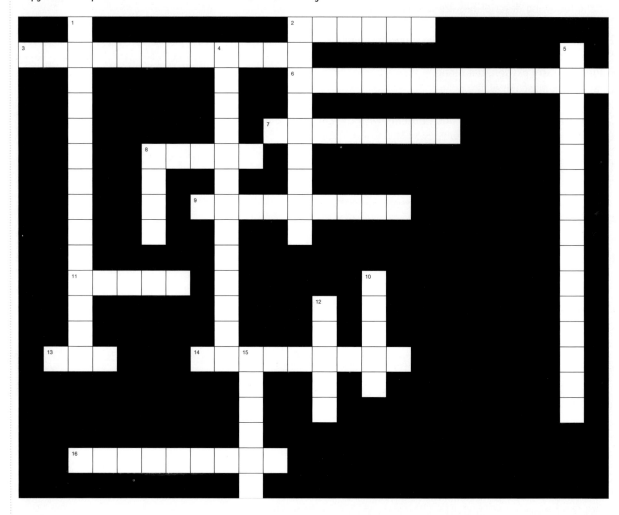

Figure 3.12 The cardiovascular system

Across:

2 What type of circulatory systems do humans have? (6)
3 What is being defined? 'The amount of blood leaving the heart per beat' (6,6)
6 If I increased stroke volume, what else will increase? (7,6)
7 Main vein in the body, brings blood back to the heart (4,4)
8 What is the name of the structure that stops blood flowing the wrong way? (5)
9 What happens to the heart rate during exercise? (9)
11 The chambers in the top half of the heart (5)
13 Which blood cells carry oxygen to help the performer work for longer? (3)
14 Which term is represented in this equation as a question mark? Cardiac output × ? = SV (5,4)
16 Which blood vessel has this characteristic? Only allows blood to pass through one cell at a time (9)

Down:

1 Found on the right side of the heart, it prevents the back flow of blood (9,5)
2 What happens to the resting heart rate as a result of regular training? (9)
4 The strongest of the muscular walls around the chambers of the heart (4,9)
5 Takes deoxygenated blood away from the heart (9,6)
8 Which blood vessel has very thin walls? (4)
10 Which blood cells protect the performer from infection? (5)
12 Takes oxygenated blood away from the heart (5)
15 Which blood vessel has a thick muscular wall? (6)

PRACTICE QUESTIONS

1. Explain why the left ventricle wall is more muscular than that of the right ventricle.

2. Explain, using the equation for cardiac output, why performers with a higher level of cardiovascular fitness have a lower resting heart rate than those with lower fitness levels.

3. An average blood pressure reading is 120/80 mmHg. Explain why two numbers are stated for blood pressure.

4. Explain why veins need to have valves.

5. Explain the importance of white blood cells to a performer.

Study hints

Try to make sure you do not confuse stroke volume and cardiac output. Try to think of stroke volume as a single stroke/beat of the heart. Cardiac output relates to the total output from the heart in one minute.

Summary

- The cardiovascular system is responsible for the transport of gases and nutrients, blood clotting and the regulation of body temperature.
- The structure of the heart allows it to complete its function to circulate blood to the body and the lungs.
- Each type of blood vessel, (arteries, capillaries, veins), has a different function.
- Vascular shunting allows the redistribution of blood flow.
- Each component of the blood (red and white cells, plasma and platelets) has a specific function.

Useful websites

Cardiovascular system
https://www.bupa.co.uk/health-information/Directory/T/
the-cardiovascular-system

Blood
www.texasheart.org/HIC/Anatomy/blood.cfm

Cardiovascular system
www.innerbody.com/image/cardov.html

Learning goals

By the end of this chapter you should be able to:

- state the composition of inhaled and exhaled air and explain the impact of physical activity on the composition of exhaled air
- identify the positions of the components of the respiratory system
- explain the role of the main components of the respiratory system in movement of oxygen and carbon dioxide into and out of the body
- explain the process of gas exchange to meet the demands of varying intensities of exercise
- describe vital capacity and tidal volume and the effect of exercise on them.

In the previous chapter we looked at the importance of the circulatory system in transporting blood carrying oxygen to our working muscles (and the rest of the body). The respiratory system is also vital to the performer, because without it the performer would not be able to receive air (containing oxygen) into the body for the circulatory system to circulate, nor would it be able to expel carbon dioxide from the body. These are the main functions of the lungs.

Key words

Inhaled air – air we breathe into the lungs

Exhaled air – air we breathe out of the lungs

Composition of inspired and expired air

Figure 4.1 shows the relative percentages of gases in the air we breathe in.

As you can see from Figure 4.1, the air we breathe in is approximately 78 per cent nitrogen, 21 per cent oxygen and 0.03 per cent carbon dioxide. Traces of water vapour are also present, but the figure will vary depending on the weather. (Not surprisingly, if it is raining there is more water vapour

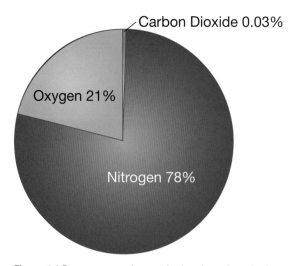

Figure 4.1 Percentages of gases in the air we breathe in

in the air.) For your course you need to know if any of these values change and, if they do, the reason why they change.

There are some traces of other gases in air as well, but these are in very small amounts (and not on your course). It is useful to know they exist though, as this explains why, when you add up the percentages of oxygen, carbon dioxide and nitrogen in air, they do not equal 100 per cent. The missing points of a percentage are due to the traces of these other gases.

We all need oxygen to release energy, but when participating in physical activity we need more, because we need more energy. The efficiency of the respiratory system in getting oxygen into the body and the circulatory system in delivering it where it is needed, will have a big impact on the level of performance achieved in most sporting activities. For example, imagine the 1500 metre runner who could only walk or do a slow jog because they could not breathe enough oxygen into their bodies to provide enough energy to go any faster, or the basketball player who could sprint down the court once on a fast break, but then had to sit out of the match for ten minutes while he recovered – neither performer would be competitively successful in their sports.

Actions

From the work you have already completed, you will know that we use oxygen to release energy.
1. What do you think happens to the level of oxygen breathed out, compared with the percentage breathed in?
2. Carbon dioxide needs to be removed from the body because it is produced during exercise as part of the process that releases energy; therefore, what do you think happens to the carbon dioxide levels?
3. Nitrogen is neither used nor created by the body, so what will happen to its levels?
4. Finally, water vapour is released during the process of energy release, therefore what would you expect to happen to the level of water vapour in air that is breathed out?

Look at Table 4.1 for a comparison of the values of the gases and water vapour in air that are inhaled (breathed in) and exhaled (breathed out). Does it match your answers?

Actions

Copy Table 4.1 and complete the final column.

COMPONENT	INHALED AIR %	EXHALED AIR %	DIFFERENCE	REASON FOR DIFFERENCE
Nitrogen	78	78	Stays the same	N/A
Oxygen	21	17	Drop in value	
Carbon dioxide	0.03	4	Increase in value	
Water vapour	Varies	Saturated	Increase in value	

Table 4.1 Composition of inhaled and exhaled air

Key words

Bronchus – a part of the airway for the transfer of air into the lungs. There is a left and right bronchus, one for each lung. Together they are referred to as bronchi

Bronchioles – smaller branches off of the bronchi within the lungs

Alveoli – found at the end of the bronchioles, they are the sites of gaseous exchange

Gaseous exchange – swapping of oxygen and carbon dioxide due to a pressure gradient

Components of the respiratory system

To begin with we need to consider the components of the respiratory system and the route the air takes to reach the lungs for gas exchange to take place. Figure 4.2 is a diagram of the human respiratory system and shows the labels you need to learn.

Air enters the body by passing through the mouth and nasal passages (nose). It is much better to breathe in through the nose than the mouth because:

- the nose has a filter system to remove dust particles from the air
- it also warms the air so that it matches body temperature
- it moistens the air so that it arrives in the lungs saturated with water to aid the respiration process.

On leaving the nasal passages, the air flows into the larynx – this is the bump you can feel on your neck, where you can easily feel your pulse if you place two fingers together and gently press just to the side of it. (If you can feel a pulse, are your fingers on an artery, vein or capillary?)

After the larynx, the air goes through the trachea, into the right or left **bronchus** (if you are talking about both, the plural word is bronchi). From the **bronchi** the air travels on to the **bronchioles** and finally on to the **alveoli**.

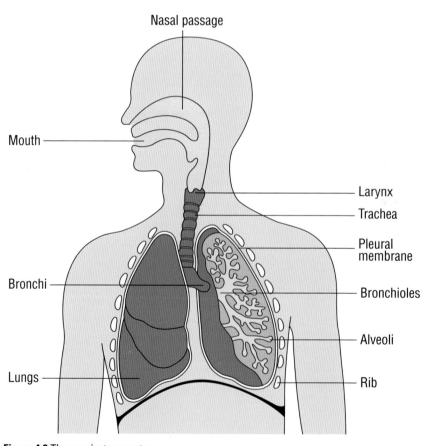

Figure 4.2 The respiratory system

The alveoli are very important; it is here that the exchange of gases takes place. Gaseous exchange is the swapping of oxygen and carbon dioxide due to the pressure gradients of each of the gases at the site of the exchange. For example, the percentage of oxygen in the lungs is much higher than that in the blood vessels arriving at the lungs. Due to the pressure difference (gradient), the oxygen diffuses from the lungs to the blood. Meanwhile, the percentage of carbon dioxide in the blood is higher than that in the lungs and so this gas diffuses from the blood to the lungs. The gases are therefore 'swapped'.

Regular endurance training will result in an increase in the number of alveoli present in the lungs and an increase in the number of capillaries that are available to exchange gases with them.

An increase in alveoli means that the performer can diffuse more oxygen into the blood, provided that the alveoli have access to a blood supply for the exchange of gases (see Figure 4.3). This is why there is an increase in the number of capillaries available. These two factors combined will lead to greater oxygen uptake during exercise and therefore potentially more oxygen available to release energy, helping to fuel exercise for longer.

Expiration and inspiration

We have seen the path that the air must take to get to the lungs, but what do we physically do to help us breathe in and out? The movement of the diaphragm and the ribs helps the movement of air into and out of the lungs.

During expiration (breathing out), the lungs slightly deflate (like a balloon losing some of the air inside it); when this happens the lungs do not take

Key words

Expiration – breathing out
Inspiration – breathing in

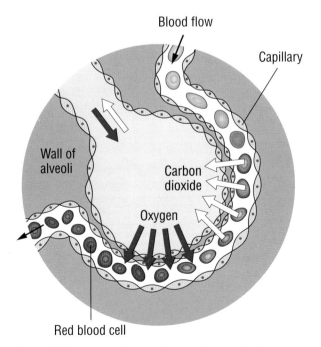

Figure 4.3 Oxygen can be seen leaving the alveolus (singular of alveoli) and carbon dioxide entering the blood

Figure 4.4 Endurance athletes have very efficient respiratory systems so that oxygen can be used in energy production for longer

Check your understanding

2. Label the two components of the respiratory system labelled A and B in Figure 4.5.

3. What is gaseous exchange?

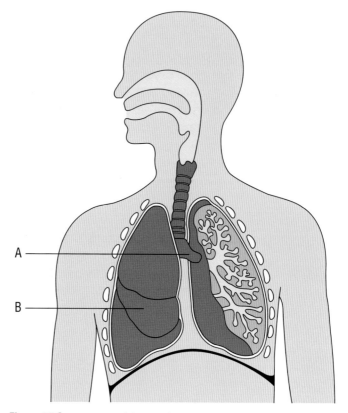

Figure 4.5 Components of the respiratory system

up as much room and so the ribs can move downwards and inwards and the diaphragm can relax (move up). This helps the lungs to expel some of the air inside them.

During inspiration (breathing in) however, the lungs need to expand so they can hold more air, like a balloon being inflated. In order to make room for the lungs to do this, the diaphragm contracts (this pulls it tight and flat, see Figure 4.6) and the ribs move up and out due to the contraction of the external intercostal muscles (these attach one rib to the rib below it – the muscle runs downwards from the upper rib and forwards to the rib below).

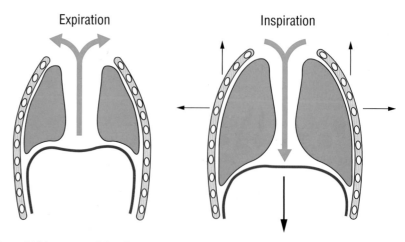

Figure 4.6 Movement of the ribs and diaphragm during expiration and inspiration

During exercise, the ventilation rate increases: an average adult male will inspire and expire between 10 to 14 times a minute at rest, but this can increase to 25 times a minute during heavy exercise. Try measuring your breathing rate by placing your hands across your chest (opposite hand to opposite shoulder) and counting the rise and fall of the rib cage. It is difficult to count accurately, but you should be able to feel a difference while at rest and immediately after exercise.

Lung volumes

The average adult human can hold about six litres of air in their lungs.

Although the lungs do not respond to regular training, for example, they do not increase in size; intensive exercise will fatigue the diaphragm and the external intercostal muscles so that they adapt and become stronger and more able to cope with the work a sports performer is doing. Due to the increased strength of these muscles, tidal volume can be increased.

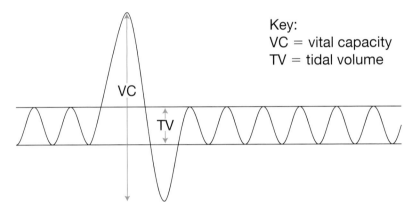

Key:
VC = vital capacity
TV = tidal volume

Figure 4.7 Vital capacity and tidal volume of a performer at rest

Figure 4.8 Changing levels of oxygen and carbon dioxide during exercise

Check your understanding

4. Why are we able to take more air into the lungs during inspiration?

5. What would you expect to happen to the lines for tidal volume in Figure 4.7 once the performer started to exercise?

Key words

Tidal volume – is the movement of air into or out of the lungs in one normal breath

Vital capacity – is the maximum amount of air that can be expired after a maximal inspiration

Actions

Shade in the containers of oxygen and carbon dioxide in Figure 4.8 to show what happens to the quantities of these gases as blood circulates around the athlete's body during exercise. The containers are numbered; number 1 is at the lungs, number 2 part way around the circulation and so on until the blood has completed its circuit back to the lungs at number 6.

PRACTICE QUESTIONS

1. Explain why the composition of air varies between that inhaled and exhaled during exercise.

2. Label the two components of the respiratory system labelled A and B in Figure 4.9.

3. Explain why inspiration rate increases as a result of exercise.

4. Explain why we need gaseous exchange to take place at the lungs and the muscles.

5. Define the term vital capacity.

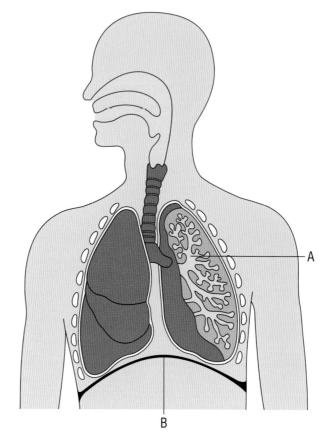

Figure 4.9 Components of the respiratory system

Summary

- The respiratory system is responsible for the movement of air containing oxygen into and out of the body.
- The composition of inhaled and exhaled air differs in relation to the amount of oxygen and carbon dioxide it contains.
- The alveoli allow gas exchange at the lungs.
- Exercise increases tidal volume.

Useful websites
Respiratory system: facts, functions and diseases
www.livescience.com/22616-respiratory-system.html

The respiratory system
www.bbc.co.uk/education/guides/z6h4jxs

The respiratory system
https://www.youtube.com/watch?v=hc1YtXc_84A

Chapter 5 Aerobic and anaerobic exercise

Learning goals

By the end of this chapter you should be able to:

- explain the difference between aerobic and anaerobic activity
- explain the energy equation during aerobic respiration
- explain why lactic acid is produced during anaerobic respiration
- explain the different energy sources for aerobic and anaerobic activity.

Aerobic and anaerobic activity

You need to understand the difference between these two terms to help you understand the way that your body generates energy for your activity.

In simple terms, aerobic means 'with oxygen', therefore anaerobic means 'without oxygen'. These terms relate to the intensity of the activity, or how hard you are physically making the body work. For example, the 100 metre sprint is an anaerobic activity because you work as hard as you can (maximal level).

When we work at this rate it is not possible to supply the muscles with the oxygen they need to release energy for the exercise, so we work without oxygen, anaerobically, and repay the oxygen debt once the exercise is completed (see below). The problem is that because of the lack of oxygen, we can only work at this level for a limited period of time, therefore longer events such as the 3000 metres are mainly aerobic.

An extreme example of an anaerobic activity is the 100 metre sprint. An extreme example of an aerobic activity is the marathon, although aspects of the marathon will be anaerobic, for example the sprint finish. Similarly, many team games will have aspects of aerobic and anaerobic activity within them, so depending on what you are physically doing in the game will depend whether you are working aerobically or anaerobically.

EVENT	PREDICTED TIME IF THE SAME PACE COULD BE MAINTAINED ANAEROBICALLY THROUGHOUT THE EVENT
100 m	10 seconds
200 m	20 seconds
400 m	40 seconds
800 m	1 minute 20 seconds
1500 m	2 minutes 30 seconds
3000 m	???

Table 5.1 Applying anaerobic rates

Key words

Aerobic – with oxygen

Anaerobic – without oxygen

Anaerobic activity – short duration, high-intensity exercise, for example, serving an 'ace' in tennis or running 100 m

Oxygen debt – the shortfall of oxygen during exercise that must be 'repaid' during recovery

Aerobic activity – long duration, medium-intensity exercise, for example playing a team game over a long period of time, such as a 90-minute football match

Actions

If it takes an elite male 100m runner approximately ten seconds to run the 100m, how long would it take an elite 3000m runner to complete their event if they were able to work at the same anaerobic pace as the 100m runner for the whole race? (See Table 5.1.) Why does it take elite athletes in the 3000m so much longer to complete their race than the time suggested through this calculation?

Actions

Look at the data in the table below, when do the events appear to change from anaerobic to aerobic?

EVENT	PREDICTED TIME IF THE SAME PACE COULD BE MAINTAINED ANAEROBICALLY THROUGHOUT THE EVENT	CURRENT WORLD RECORD TO NEAREST SECOND (MEN)
100 m	10 seconds	10 seconds
200 m	20 seconds	19 seconds
400 m	40 seconds	43 seconds
800 m	1 minute 20 seconds	1 min 41 seconds
1500 m	2 minutes 30 seconds	3 minutes 26 seconds
3000 m	???	7 minutes 21 seconds

Table 5.2 From anaerobic exercise to aerobic

Check your understanding

1. Copy and complete Table 5.3 by stating if the described activity will use mainly aerobic or anaerobic respiration

Activity	Aerobic or anaerobic?
100m sprint	
4 × 100 m women's relay	
1500m	
Sprint finish in 3000 m	
Racing dive to start a race in swimming	
Throwing a discus	
Playing a long set in tennis	

Table 5.3 Which activities are aerobic, which are anaerobic?

Key word

Aerobic respiration – production of energy using oxygen

Aerobic respiration

We have seen from the previous chapters that the body needs oxygen to function and more is needed when we exercise. What is the reason for this?

In order for us to do any physical work, we need energy. This energy comes from the food we eat. Energy can be released using oxygen (aerobic) or without using oxygen (anaerobic).

Aerobic activities are activities where you do not work flat out or maximally, but instead you tend to have to work for longer periods of time. More energy is released if oxygen is present, therefore in aerobic activities the more oxygen supplied to the tissues, the better as this allows the athlete to maintain a good work rate for longer.

Glucose (from carbohydrates) is broken down in our tissues in the presence of oxygen to release energy. This is represented by the equation shown in Figure 5.1.

$$C_6H_{12}O_6 + 6O_2 \Rightarrow \text{Gives} \quad 6CO_2 + 6H_2O + \text{Energy}$$

Glucose   Oxygen   Carbon dioxide   Water

Figure 5.1 Energy equation during aerobic respiration

During aerobic respiration:
- energy is released from respiration
- glucose is needed
- oxygen is needed
- carbon dioxide is produced
- water is produced.

By looking at this equation we can see why:
- oxygen levels go down
- carbon dioxide levels go up
- levels of water vapour increase.

Anaerobic respiration

If the level of exercise is too intense, for example in the 100m, oxygen cannot be supplied quickly enough to release energy aerobically. When this happens, we release energy anaerobically, without oxygen. We can only produce energy anaerobically for a relatively short period of time because a by-product of working anaerobically is lactic acid.

If oxygen is present, lactic acid can be broken down (into carbon dioxide and water) and breathed out of the body. However, if there is insufficient oxygen the lactate will begin to accumulate in the blood. This causes an increased acidity in the muscle cells and blood. As a result, the muscle becomes fatigued, therefore the performer needs to slow down or stop in order to recover before continuing at the same intensity of physical work. For example, a sprinter doing interval training will complete their sprint and stop, allowing themselves time to recover before completing another set. Games players who have just sprinted for the ball to reach it before their opponent will recover by jogging back into position, once they have passed on the ball.

During this recovery period the performer will still be breathing heavily, even though they are not working hard. This is so they can take in enough additional oxygen to repay the oxygen debt they have developed. An oxygen debt is the amount of oxygen consumed during recovery, above

Actions

Analyse the equation. Write as many statements as you can from the information presented in the equation, for example, what do you need to add together to give you energy? Check your understanding by looking at the points below.

Check your understanding

2. Why do carbon dioxide levels go up as a result of aerobic respiration?

3. What happens to the amount of water vapour breathed out compared to that breathed in during aerobic respiration?

Key words

Anaerobic respiration – production of energy without using oxygen

Lactic acid – a by-product of anaerobic respiration

By-product – something additional that is made during a process, for example, lactic acid during anaerobic energy production

that which would normally have been used at rest; it results from a shortfall in availability of oxygen during exercise. This additional oxygen is used to restock oxygen levels in the muscles and tissues, and to help break down any lactic acid that has formed.

Energy sources

Further information can be found about diet and nutrition in Chapter 16. The focus here is on our main sources of energy.

The more physical work we do, the more energy we need to complete it. As we have seen earlier, we can produce energy aerobically or anaerobically. In the case of aerobic respiration, the energy equation shows us that we need to combine glucose with oxygen to produce energy, but where does this glucose come from?

The food we eat contains different nutrients. Some of these nutrients can be broken down to release energy. Fats and carbohydrates are our main sources of energy. Carbohydrates can be found in foods containing starch, for example bread, pasta and rice, while fats can be found in dairy products such as milk, cheese and butter.

When we eat, each nutrient is broken down further by the digestive system. For the purposes of this qualification you need to remember that fats are broken down and used as a fuel source for aerobic activity and that carbohydrates can be broken down and used for aerobic and anaerobic respiration.

Carbohydrates can only be stored in limited quantities in the body. Carbohydrates are broken down into glucose and enter the circulatory system. Some of this glucose is absorbed by the muscle cells and is therefore readily available for use. Any excess glucose is converted to fat and stored in the body.

Fat will provide most of the energy the body requires while at rest. Fat is broken down into fatty acids or glycerol. The fatty acids can be broken down to produce glucose. Fats are the slowest source of energy as they are slow to digest and convert into a usable form of energy, but they are the most energy efficient, providing more energy for exercise. Because they are slow to break down and take large quantities of oxygen to do so, they are not used in anaerobic activity but are very important in endurance activities such as marathons.

PRACTICE QUESTIONS

1. Give an example from a game situation when you would be working aerobically and another example when you would be working anaerobically.

2. Name the gas that increases in quantity as a result of aerobic respiration.

3. Describe the aerobic energy equation.

4. Why does lactic acid build up in muscle tissue and what is the impact of this on performance?

5. Explain why fats are not used in anaerobic respiration.

Summary

- Activity can be aerobic or anaerobic.
- Energy production can be aerobic or anaerobic.
- Fats are used in aerobic respiration for aerobic activity.
- Carbohydrates are used in anaerobic respiration for anaerobic activity.

Useful websites

Aerobic and anaerobic energy systems
www.pponline.co.uk/encyc/aerobic-and-anaerobic-energy-systems-39444

Aerobic and anaerobic respiration
www.bbc.co.uk/schools/gcsebitesize/science/add_aqa/respiration/respirationrev3.shtml

The truth about carbs
www.nhs.uk/livewell/loseweight/pages/the-truth-about-carbs.aspx

Chapter 6 Short-term effects of exercise

Learning goals
By the end of this chapter you should be able to:
- explain the short-term effects of exercise on the muscular system
- explain the short-term effects of exercise on the cardiovascular system
- explain the short-term effects of exercise on the respiratory system.

In the first four chapters of this book we learnt about the four body systems and how they are necessary to allow us to exercise, but what effect does exercise have on these systems? How does our body respond to exercise?

Actions

Take part in physical activity for a couple of minutes (for example skipping, jumping, running up and down stairs), or think back to the last time you had a practical session. What were the immediate effects of exercise that you noticed? Can you think of an immediate effect to record in each of the spaces in Table 6.1? Copy and complete Table 6.1.

Body system	Short-term effect of exercise
Muscular	
Cardiovascular	
Respiratory	

Table 6.1 Short-term effects of exercise

Key words

Short-term effects – something that doesn't last for very long, for example, being out of breath after running, but after a few minutes breathing returns to normal

Adaptations – changes made to the body as a result of regular training, for example, an increase in strength is a training adaptation

For your course you need to think of the short-term effects of exercise and the long-term training effects or adaptations resulting from regular exercise. It is important you understand the difference between the two. The short-term effects are exactly that, once you stop exercise any effects that you felt reduce. For example, if your heart rate increased as an effect of exercise once you stop exercising it would slowly drop back to your heart rate before you started exercising. The effects don't last; they are only short-term.

Long-term training effects are those that cause the body to adapt. They take a lot of training (training over a number of weeks, long term) and the effects on the body will last a longer period of time (as long as you maintain regular training). These effects are covered in more detail in Chapter 12.

Short-term effects of exercise

As soon as you take part in physical activity your body experiences some immediate effects. These are changes that take place on a temporary basis straight away to give immediate help, so that you can try to complete the work you are asking of your body. There will be changes to heart rate, breathing rate and body temperature, for example. Heart rate increases to speed up oxygen delivery to the muscles, while the breathing rate increases to take in more air containing oxygen and to remove increased levels of carbon dioxide. Once exercise has stopped your body will slowly return back to its pre-exercise state in terms of heart rate, breathing rate and body temperature.

Check your understanding

1. What is the difference between a short-term and long-term effect of exercise?

Short-term effects of exercise on the muscular system

As soon as you take part in physical activity your muscular system experiences some immediate effects related to that exercise. The immediate changes to the muscular system are:

- increased demand for energy for muscular work
- increased carbon dioxide production
- increased temperature
- lactic acid production
- lactate accumulation
- muscle fatigue.

So why do these things happen? In order to carry out any movement we need energy, therefore if we move more (than when at rest) our muscles will need more energy to complete the tasks. We saw in the previous chapter that energy can be provided aerobically or anaerobically, using fats or carbohydrates as a source of fuel for energy production. If our body produces energy aerobically using oxygen we know that carbon dioxide is produced. Therefore, if we need to produce more energy we will also be producing more carbon dioxide.

$$\underset{\text{Glucose}}{C_6H_{12}O_6} + \underset{\text{Oxygen}}{6O_2} \xrightarrow{\text{Gives}} \underset{\text{Carbon dioxide}}{6CO_2} + \underset{\text{Water}}{6H_2O} + \text{Energy}$$

Figure 6.1 Production of carbon dioxide during aerobic respiration

Some of the energy that is produced is heat energy; this is why our temperature increases when we exercise. Have you noticed how you might be cold at the start of a PE lesson, but as soon as you start moving you warm up? This is due to the heat that your body generates.

Key word

Lactate – formed from lactic acid

So far we have talked about providing energy aerobically with oxygen. What happens to the muscles if there is insufficient oxygen? If you study Chemistry or go on to further study, you may go into the detail of how lactate or lactic acid is produced, but for this course it is enough to know that in the absence of oxygen lactic acid can be produced when generating energy anaerobically. If oxygen is available, lactic acid can be broken down as soon as it forms. If oxygen is not available, lactic acid is converted to lactate, which then diffuses from the muscle and accumulates in the blood.

Key word

Muscle fatigue – drop in ability of the muscle to carry out physical work due to lack of energy

Check your understanding

2. Name two by-products of aerobic respiration in the production of energy.

3. How do the short-term responses to exercise help the cardiovascular system fulfil its role?

The increased acidity of the blood (due in part to the accumulating lactate) interferes with muscular contraction, making our muscles feel tired.

Short-term effects of exercise on the cardiovascular system

Short-term effects on the cardiovascular system also occur in response to exercise to try to help the body meet the demands of the extra physical work. Before looking at the short-term effects it may be worth revisiting Chapter 3 on the cardiovascular system to remind yourself of the meanings of each of the terms in the list below.

The immediate changes to the cardiovascular system are:

- heart rate increases
- increased stroke volume
- increased cardiac output
- blood pressure increases
- vascular shunting takes place.

Our heart rate increases in order to increase blood flow. At rest approximately 5.5 litres of blood will flow around the body per minute, but this can be increased to approximately 30 litres during exercise. Remember, it is not that there is more blood, it is just that what there is is circulating much more quickly. The increase in the volume of blood being circulated is due to an increase in heart rate and an increase in stroke volume, giving us a greater cardiac output during exercise.

$$\text{Cardiac output} = \text{stroke volume} \times \text{heart rate}$$

Our blood pressure increases temporarily because blood is being forced out of the heart more quickly due to the increased blood flow as a result of a higher heart rate.

Remember in Chapter 3 we looked at vascular shunting and the reasons for it. It is a short-term effect of exercise to make sure there is enough blood circulating our bodies to carry out the functions the body needs, for example, transport of nutrients, temperature regulation and oxygen/carbon dioxide transport. When we exercise the body vasoconstricts the blood vessels supplying the digestive system. This doesn't stop all blood flow to the digestive system otherwise this would damage the cells. But vasoconstriction does reduce blood flow so only essential actions can be carried out and vasodilates the blood vessels going to the active muscles so that nutrients and oxygen can be delivered for energy production and carbon dioxide can be removed. Look at Figure 6.2 – note the changes in percentage of blood flow to the different areas of the body at rest and during exercise.

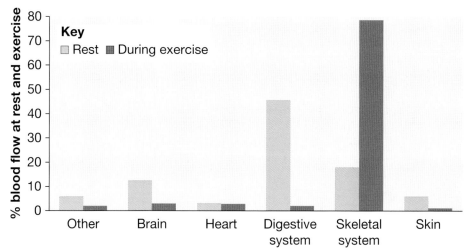

Figure 6.2 Variation in blood flow at rest compared to during exercise.

Check your understanding

4. What would the cardiac output be for an individual with the following resting and exercise heart rate and stroke volume values?

	At rest	During exercise
Stroke volume (ml/beat)	68 ml/beat	120 ml/beat
Heart rate (bpm)	75 beats/min	175 beats/min

Short-term effects of exercise on the respiratory system

The respiratory system will also undergo short-term changes as a result of exercise. The immediate changes to the respiratory system are:

- increased breathing/ventilation rate
- increased depth of breathing
- oxygen debt.

Our breathing rate increases so that we can take more oxygen into the lungs and also so we can expel carbon dioxide, as it is not needed by the body. In addition to breathing more quickly, we can take deeper breaths. This has the same effect, in that this allows us to increase the amount of oxygen we can take in and then transfer to the working muscles so they have the required energy to work.

Recovery rates

One of the immediate effects of exercise is an increase in heart rate. A person's recovery rate is the amount of time it takes for their heart rate to return back to its resting rate after they have finished exercising. The reason the heart rate remains high is that it is continuing to deliver an increased amount of oxygen to the muscles (this is called paying back the oxygen debt) to reduce lactic acid and lactate content and to transport carbon dioxide to the lungs. The quicker your heart rate returns to its

Actions

Copy and fill in the boxes in Figure 6.3 to explain an immediate effect of exercise on the system indicated in the boxes and how this supports the performer when exercising.

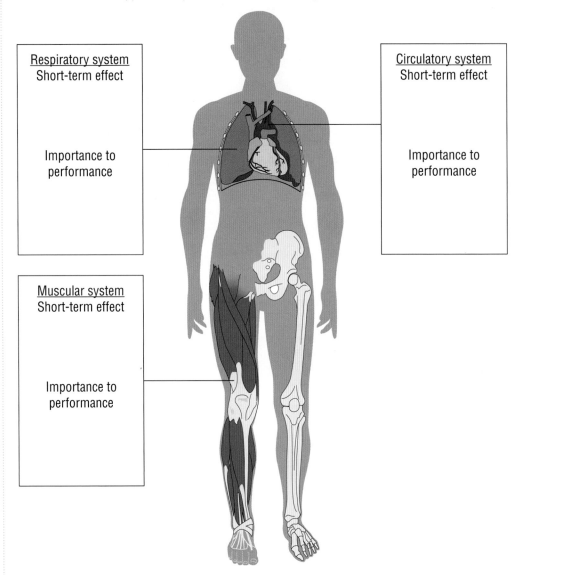

Respiratory system
Short-term effect

Importance to performance

Circulatory system
Short-term effect

Importance to performance

Muscular system
Short-term effect

Importance to performance

Figure 6.3 Immediate effects of exercise on the body systems

resting value the fitter you are thought to be. Note how the body systems have to work together to recover from exercise, for example, the cardio-respiratory and the muscular system. Due to the period of exercise the muscles have a shortage of oxygen and too much lactate. This means that oxygen is needed to help break the lactate down into carbon dioxide and water (see Chapter 5). The oxygen to do this can only be supplied to the muscle via the blood stream, so the heart rate remains high to keep pumping blood containing oxygen to the muscles. However, unless the respiratory rate also remains high there will not be enough oxygen taken into the lungs to be transported to the blood and then to the muscles to help them recover. Once oxygen stores have been replenished in the muscles and the lactic acid and lactate broken down, breathing rate and heart rate can return to resting levels.

Actions

How long does it take you to recover from exercise? Copy the graph in Figure 6.4. Take your resting heart rate and plot it on the graph. Take part in some aerobic exercise for five minutes. At the end of the exercise, take your heart rate again and plot on the graph. Continue to take your heart rate every minute until it is back to your resting level. Compare your heart rate values with others' in your group. Whose heart rate returned to resting the quickest? Does this mean that that person is the fittest, or is there another reason for the differences in heart rate?

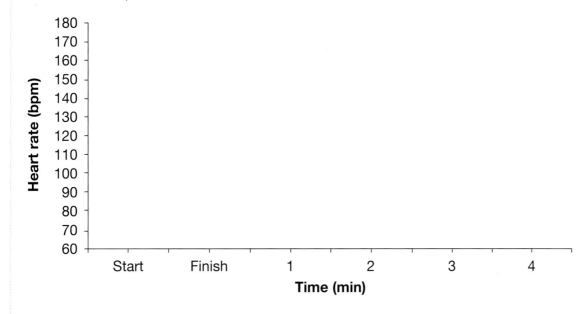

Figure 6.4 Graph showing heart rate values in bpm

PRACTICE QUESTIONS

1. Explain why there is an increased need for oxygen in the muscles during exercise.

2. Explain why we experience an increase in temperature as a result of exercise.

3. Explain why lactate accumulates in the blood.

4. Analyse, using the graph in Figure 6.2, the effect of exercise on redistribution of blood flow during exercise compared to rest.

5. Describe how the body systems work together to allow the body to exercise.

5. Why does the heart rate remain high even after exercise has stopped?

Study hints

Question 5 makes reference to body systems working together. In your answer you would need to make sure you referenced more than one body system and described the link between them.

Summary

- An exercise session will have short-term effects on:
  - the muscular system
  - the cardiovascular system
  - the respiratory system.
- These three body systems work together to allow exercise and to recover from it.

Useful websites

The cardiovascular system and exercise
www.sport-fitness-advisor.com/cardiovascular-system-and-exercise.html

The short- and long-terms effect of exercise on the cardiovascular system
www.ehow.co.uk/list_6524144_short-effects-exercise-cardiovascular-system.html

The effects of exercise
www.s-cool.co.uk/gcse/pe/how-the-body-obtains-its-energy/revise-it/the-effects-of-exercise

Chapter 7 Movement analysis – lever systems in sport and physical activity

Learning goals

By the end of this chapter you should be able to:

- identify and describe the use of first class lever systems
- identify and describe the use of second class lever systems
- identify and describe the use of third class lever systems
- explain the mechanical advantage of lever systems
- explain the disadvantage of lever systems
- analyse the use of lever systems in physical activity.

Lever systems in the body

Levers are normally used to make physical work easier, for example, to make it easier to move something that is heavy, or to move something quickly. When we exercise most of our movements will involve the use of levers. For example, when we run, lift weights, kick or throw a ball, all of these actions will involve the use of levers. A lever system within the body would use a lever (bone) to move an object, for example, when we run we are the object being moved, but when kicking a ball, the object being moved is the ball.

All lever systems are made up of four components:

- the load
- the fulcrum
- the effort
- the lever.

The load is the object requiring moving, the effort is the muscular force we use to move the object, the fulcrum is the joint around which the movement occurs and the bones of the skeleton are the levers. If asked to sketch a diagram of a lever system, you would need to include all four parts.

To get the idea, we can use non-sporting examples of lever systems:

A. Imagine a road is blocked with a fallen tree. A tree would be too heavy to lift, but a person could move the tree a little by using a lever system. By placing one end of a long length of wood under the fallen tree and then pushing down on the other end of the wood, the fallen tree could be moved.

B. Wheelbarrows are used to move heavy objects more easily. The heavy object is placed in the wheelbarrow and then the handles lifted to push the wheelbarrow containing the heavy object.

> ### Actions
> Identify the components of the lever systems in examples A and B.

Key words

Lever systems – created in the body by the musculo-skeletal system

Components of a lever system – the parts that make up a lever system, for example, in the body this would be a bone, a joint, a muscle and the body weight

The difference between each lever system is the order in which these components are arranged.

Actions

Look at the components of a lever system. Ignoring the lever (as this remains constant) rearrange the remaining three components three times so that a different component is in the middle each time.

Hopefully you arrived at the following list:
- Load, Fulcrum, Effort
- Effort, Load, Fulcrum
- Fulcrum, Effort, Load

Don't worry if your list isn't identical to this one. Provided each of your examples contains all three components and has a different part of the lever system in the middle – these are the three classes of lever systems.

Lever systems have standard symbols that are used to represent each part. You will need to know these standard symbols.

Load

Fulcrum

Effort

Lever

Figure 7.1 Components of a lever system

Actions

Rearrange the components of the lever system in the sketch in Figure 7.2 and sketch two more possible lever systems. How do your sketches match up with the images of the lever systems below?

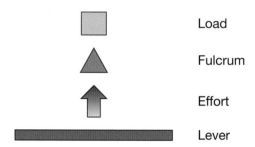

Figure 7.2 Sketch of a lever system

Check your understanding

1. Name the components of a lever system.

First class levers

First class lever systems are arranged so that the fulcrum is between the effort and the load (see Figure 7.2). This is the arrangement of a first class lever system. Example A (see p. 49) of the fallen tree would use a first class lever system: the tree would be the load, the end of the wooden bar under the tree would be the fulcrum and the effort would be the muscular force applied to the other end of the wooden bar. If you were to sketch this lever system, which way would the arrow, that represents the effort, point?

There are a limited number of examples of first class lever systems in the body. In the examples of levers given so far it has been clear to see where the effort is applied in relation to the other parts of the lever system. However, this is not always as clear when we look at lever systems within the body. For example, due to where the triceps attach to the elbow joint, elbow extension is considered to be use of a first class lever system. Further explanation of this can be left for level 3 Sport or PE courses; it is sufficient for you to appreciate that elbow extension involves a first class lever. (The elbow is the fulcrum, the effort is provided by the triceps due to their insertion point at the elbow and the load is whatever is being thrown, for example a javelin). Nodding of the head is another example of a first class lever system, important in sport when watching the flight of a ball for example; in this example the load would be the weight of the head.

Second class levers

The components of the second class lever system are arranged as shown in Figure 7.3. What component is at the centre of this lever system?

Again there are limited examples of these lever systems in the body. The one with possibly the greatest application for sport is the second class lever system formed between the ball of the foot, the gastrocnemius and the load of the bodyweight as we point our toes, or go onto our toes (the foot is the lever bar).

Actions

Copy Figure 7.3. Add label lines to show the parts of the body that take on the role of each of the lever's components.

Third class levers

The final class of lever is shown in Figure 7.4. What is the component in the middle of this lever system?

One way to remember the difference between each system is to remember the component in the middle of each one. A popular method is 1-2-3 = F-L-E. You can tell when it's a first class lever system as the fulcrum is in-between the other components; in the second class it is the load and in the third it is the effort.

Third class lever systems are the most common in the body and therefore are involved in a lot of our movements. For example, a biceps curl uses a third class lever system, as does hitting a ball with a racket or bat, or at the knee when we kick a ball, or the hip when we run.

Actions

Find three photographs (for example from the internet or newspaper) of different sports performers 'in action'. Stick each image onto a larger sheet of paper and annotate each image to show the position of at least one lever system.

Check your understanding

2. Identify the components of the first class lever system in the nodding action of the head.

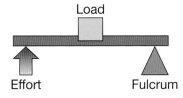

Figure 7.3. Second class lever system

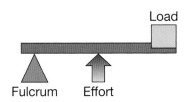

Figure 7.4 Third class lever system

Figure 7.5 Third class lever systems in use as the player moves the knee and hip in preparation for a shot

Figure 7.6 A third class lever system in use to strike the tennis ball

Mechanical advantage and disadvantage

Lever systems can be used to:

- move a heavier load
- move a load further and faster.

Lever systems that let you lift a heavier load are said to provide a mechanical advantage. For example, a car jack will only lift a car a short distance, but requires relatively little effort to move it all at. These levers are slower but used where strength is a priority.

Lever systems where a greater force needs to be applied than the load to be moved is said to provide a mechanical disadvantage. However, these levers are of use to us in sport as they allow us to move the load a large distance, with a large range of motion. Think of a tennis forehand, or a drive in badminton, think of the speed that can be generated in the racket head and the impact this has on the level of difficulty to return the shot.

The position of each part of the lever system relative to each other will determine whether the lever has a mechanical advantage and can be used to lift heavy loads or a disadvantage where greater effort is needed but the load can be moved a greater distance and with speed.

Actions

Go back to Figures 7.2, 7.3 and 7.4 of the different classes of lever system. Which lever system has the effort further than the load from the fulcrum? This class of lever is said to have a mechanical advantage. Which lever system has the effort nearer than the load to the fulcrum? This class of lever system is said to operate at a mechanical disadvantage (due to the effort required to move the load).

Actions

Take part in a weight or fitness circuit training session. Analyse the movements at each station and identify a different exercise that uses each one of the lever systems. Copy and complete Table 7.1 below.

	Description of station	Sketch system being used	Mechanical advantage	Mechanical disadvantage
First class				
Second class				
Third class				

Table 7.1 The use of lever systems in physical activity

PRACTICE QUESTIONS

1. Which class of lever system will sports performers use the most when participating in physical activity?

2. State the two functions of levers.

3. Identify the class of lever and the components of the lever system in use during a biceps curl.

4. Figure 7.7 shows a diver preparing to leave the starting blocks and a close up of the foot position once the signal to start has been given.

Analyse the role of the second class lever system as the diver leaves the starting blocks.

Figure 7.7 Use of second class lever system in sport

5. Giving an example from sport and physical activity, describe mechanical advantage.

Check your understanding

4. Which lever system is said to provide a mechanical advantage?

5. Even though third class levers are said to have a mechanical disadvantage, why are they of use to sports performers?

Study hints
Remember 1-2-3 = F-L-E

Summary

- There are three classes of lever system.
- Each lever system has the following components: lever, fulcrum, effort and load.
- Third class lever systems are the most frequently occurring in the body.
- First and second class lever systems have a mechanical advantage.
- Third class lever systems operate at a mechanical disadvantage.

Useful websites

Levers
www.brianmac.co.uk/levers.htm

Lever systems
https://www.youtube.com/watch?v=qFdW679DhAk

Levers
www.technologystudent.com/forcomom/lever1.htm

Chapter 8 Movement analysis – planes and axes of movement

Learning goals

By the end of this chapter you should be able to:

- identify the body planes and axes
- describe movement in the sagittal plane about the frontal axis
- describe movement in the frontal plane about the sagittal axis
- describe movement in the transverse plane about the vertical axis
- provide examples of the movements at each plane, about each axis.

Key words

Plane – an imaginary line or flat surface that is used to divide the body

Axis – something that the body, or a body part, can rotate about

Sagittal plane – line dividing the body vertically into left and right sides

Frontal plane – line dividing the body vertically into front and back

Transverse plane – line dividing the body horizontally from front to back

We need to know about planes and axes as they allow us to analyse movement. For GCSE we need a basic understanding of planes and axes in preparation for future study at Level 3, for example A level or BTEC and later on at university.

Don't be surprised to find different terms being used for planes and axes if you look at different books or internet sources, but just make sure you learn the terminology given below for your assessment. Even though different labels may be used, they will be describing the same three planes and axes, so check the descriptions if the labels differ.

Planes of motion

Look at Figure 8.1. The body is split into three main planes. Each plane allows a specific type of movement. Many movements in sport take place

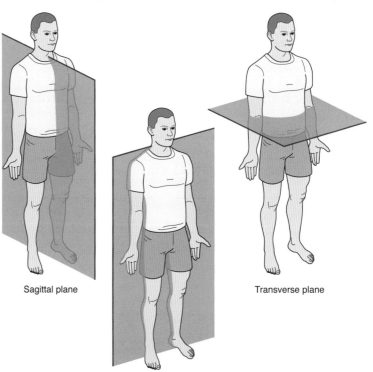

Sagittal plane

Frontal plane

Transverse plane

Figure 8.1 The planes of the body. A Sagittal plane; B Frontal plane; C Transverse plane

in multiple planes and this is something you might need to study if you go on to study planes and axes at university. For this course you only need to be aware of the three main planes and axes and the basic movement each allows.

Actions

Look at Figure 8.2. Try to imagine yourself in a very narrow corridor, just wide enough for you to fit in, so your shoulders are touching the walls of the corridor on each side. What movements could you carry out with your arms? What direction could you move your arms? What about your legs? To help imagine this, try standing sideways on to a wall or door so that your shoulder is almost touching the wall. What movements can you do with the body on the side touching the wall?

The type of movements you will have listed for this plane will be those where you bend and straighten the limb, for example, bending your arm at the elbow as though you were doing a biceps curl, or bending your leg at the knee as though you were about to kick a ball. This range of movement is flexion and extension (see Chapter 1 for a recap on movement possibilities). Therefore, the body is only able to use flexion and extension in the sagittal plane.

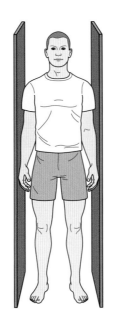

Figure 8.2 Movement in the sagittal plane

Actions

Imagine now that you are standing in a thin space between two walls, with your back against one and your chest against another. Is it possible to carry out flexion and extension? What movement possibilities are there now?

Hopefully, you will have identified abduction and adduction as the possible movements at this plane, taking parts of the body out to the side away from the body or bringing them back in again.

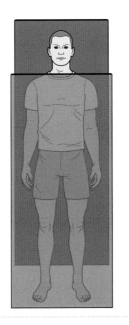

Figure 8.3 Movement in the frontal plane

Actions

Imagine now that you are standing in a giant drinks can: your body is surrounded by a ring of metal, there is no room to flex or extend your body, or to abduct or adduct. What movement possibility is left?

Movement will have been very restricted, you may have identified rotation or twisting movements. These are the types of movement that occur in the transverse plane.

Figure 8.4 Movement in the transverse plane

The major body axes

We know from Chapter 1 that in order for our bones to move, movement has to take place around a joint. Therefore, in order for these movements to take place there has to be an axis (which goes through a joint) for the bones of the skeleton to move about. For example, when we talked of a biceps curl involving flexion and extension in the sagittal plane we know this movement is only possible because of the elbow joint. In this example an axis passes through the elbow joint allowing movement around it.

Check your understanding

1. Which plane divides the body into left and right sides?

2. Which plane divides the body horizontally?

3. What are the movement possibilities in the sagittal plane?

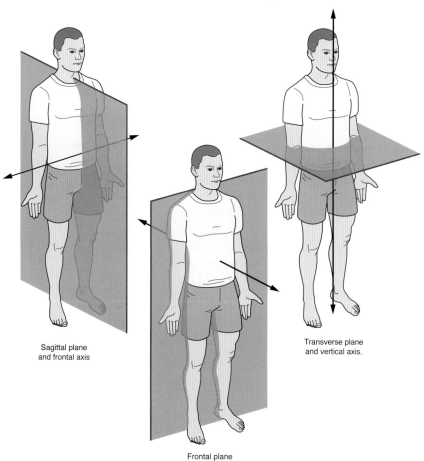

Sagittal plane
and frontal axis

Frontal plane
and sagittal axis

Transverse plane
and vertical axis.

Figure 8.5 The axes of the body

There are three main directions for axes in the body that all movements rotate around. Each axis works with a specific plane.

Actions

Take a piece of paper (half a sheet of A4 would be big enough). Using a pencil, make a hole in the middle of the paper and push the pencil until it is halfway through. (If you want to be more creative you could shape the paper to look like a person!)

A. Position the pencil so it represents the frontal axis (use Figure 8.5 to help); the piece of paper represents the body. What plane does the piece of paper represent? Look at the direction of the paper and use Figure 8.1 to help you.

Think of a high board diver in swimming; if you rotate the paper around the frontal axis, what sort of movement might the body be doing?

B. Now orientate the pencil so it represents the sagittal axis (use Figure 8.5).

What plane does the piece of paper represent? Look at the direction of the paper and use Figure 8.1 to help you. Think of a gymnast doing a floor routine, if you rotate the paper around the sagittal axis, what sort of movement might the body be doing?

C. Now orientate the pencil so it represents the vertical axis (use Figure 8.5).

What plane does the piece of paper represent? Look at the direction of the paper and use Figure 8.1 to help you. Think of a trampolinist; if you rotate the paper around the vertical axis, what sort of movement might the body be doing?

Key words

Frontal axis – line passing through the body horizontally from left to right

Sagittal axis – line passing through the body horizontally from front to back

Vertical axis – line passing through the body vertically from top to bottom

Actions

Copy and complete Table 8.1 to give a summary of the movement pattern at each plane and axis.

Plane	Axis	Movement	Example
	Frontal axis	Flexion and extension	
	Sagittal axis	Abduction and adduction	
	Vertical axis	Twisting/rotation	

Table 8.1 Summary of movement at planes at axes

4. Identify the axis that works with the sagittal plane.

5. Give an example from a game of a movement that would occur about the vertical axis.

Study hints

Remember the axis is a straight line through the body that the body part (or body) rotates around.

PRACTICE QUESTIONS

1. Identify the plane in Figure 8.6.

Figure 8.6 Planes of motion

2. A cartwheel occurs in the frontal plane. What axis is used for this movement?

3. Give an example of a movement that takes place in the transverse plane about the vertical axis.

4. Explain why it is not possible to complete a front somersault about a vertical axis.

5. Analyse the movement in Figure 8.7 to determine the plane and axis in use as the diver completes the somersault.

Figure 8.7 In which plane and about which axis does the movement take place?

Summary

- There are three major planes and axes in the body.
- All movements occur in a plane about an axis:
  - A somersault occurs in the sagittal plane about the frontal axis.
  - A cartwheel occurs in the frontal plane about the sagittal axis.
  - A full twist occurs in the transverse plane about the vertical axis.

Useful websites

Axis of movement animation
https://www.youtube.com/watch?v=iP7fpHuVaiA

Understanding planes and axes of movement (pdf)
www.physical-solutions.co.uk/wp-content/uploads/2015/05/
Understanding-Planes-and-Axes-of-Movement.pdf

Understanding exercise – planes, axes and movement
www.todaysfitnesstrainer.com/understanding-exercise-planes-axes-movement/

Chapter 9 – Physical training – health, fitness and exercise

Learning goals

By the end of this chapter you should be able to:

- define the terms:
  - fitness
  - health
  - exercise
  - performance
- discuss the relationship between these concepts
- describe the components of fitness and link them to specific sports
- assess the relative importance of the components of fitness in physical activity and sport.

There is often confusion over the difference between health and fitness. For this part of the course you need to understand these terms, define them and explain the difference between them. You also need to know the components of fitness and their importance to sporting activities.

Actions

Think about the two words health and fitness. Copy and complete Table 9.1 by listing the words that you associate with someone who is healthy or fit. Use these words to give a definition of health and another for fitness and feedback your answers to the rest of the group.

Fitness	Health

Table 9.1 Understanding health and fitness

Key word

Health – a state of complete emotional, physical and social well-being and not merely the absence of disease and infirmity

Health

There are many different definitions of health. While definitions differ slightly, they all focus on the same principles that health is not just about our physical state or being free from disease. For your course you need to learn the definition stated here in the key word, which is the same as in the glossary.

Actions

Look at Figures 9.1 and 9.2. Who do you think would be the healthiest? Can you tell from the image? Justify your answer.

Figure 9.1 Sports performers playing hurling

Figure 9.2 Non-sport performer – sedentary

People who do not take part in sport can still be healthy provided they have some form of regular physical activity and interests to help them stay healthy–socially, emotionally and physically. Through adopting a healthy lifestyle (balanced diet, regular sleep, non-smoking, limited alcohol consumption, appropriate level of physical activity), they can still maintain their health (see Chapter 15 for more information on lifestyles).

Fitness

Fitness is defined by the Edexcel examination specification as the ability to meet the demands of the environment. This means that you are able to cope with the amount of physical work you need to do.

If someone is never expected to do any more physical work than walk to the bus stop and they can do this without undue stress, then they are as 'fit' as the sports performer who trains regularly to meet the demands of their 'work'. The difference in fitness would become obvious only if the non-athlete were suddenly expected to do the same amount of physical work as the athlete. Sports performers train so they are 'fit' for their sport and the demands of their physical activity. Each athlete will be fit for their sport but not necessarily for a different one. For example, a sprinter would not perform well in a marathon and, while a marathon runner would be able to run 100 m, they would not be able to do so at the speed required by a sprinter. Therefore, they would not perform well in a sprint event.

Check your understanding

1. Name the three aspects of health in addition to being free from disease and infirmity.

Key word

Fitness – the ability to meet the demands of the environment

Actions

Look at Figures 9.3 and 9.4. Who is the fittest? Justify your answer.

Figure 9.3 Sports performers playing handball

Figure 9.4 Wheelchair athletes competing in the London marathon

Actions

Who is the fittest person in your class? How do you know they are the fittest?

When does it become obvious that they are the fittest? Is the fittest person in your class also the healthiest?

Your answer to the last part of this question may be 'yes', but equally, it may not be. It is possible to be fit while not being healthy. Can you think of an occasion when this might be the case? Many fit athletes may temporarily be unhealthy if they are suffering from a cold or similar infection, or an illness such as diabetes, or even in extreme cases the initial stages of major diseases such as cancer. An increase in fitness does improve the chances of being healthy, but it cannot guarantee good health.

Exercise

As you can see, this definition links health with fitness, recognising the benefits of physical activity – through exercise we can develop our physical, emotional and social health and our physical fitness (see Chapter 15 for more information). A detailed explanation of the effects of exercise and training on the body can be found in Chapter 12.

(see Chapter 15 for more information)

Key word

Exercise – a form of physical activity done to maintain or improve health and/or fitness; it is not competitive sport

Check your understanding

2. Define the term exercise.

Actions

Can you see any link between the terms exercise, health, fitness and performance? Discuss your ideas with a partner and feedback to the group. Annotate Figure 9.5 to help you capture some of your ideas.

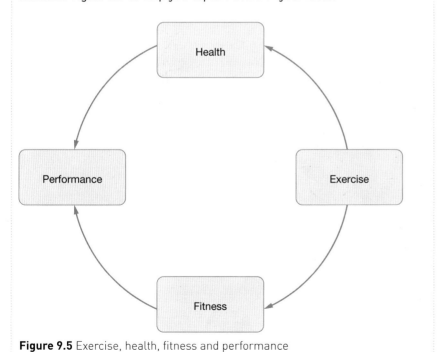

Figure 9.5 Exercise, health, fitness and performance

Performance

Performance can be anything from excellent to poor; it is simply a way of describing the quality demonstrated in a practical activity. We judge performances in gymnastics and diving and how well a task is completed has a direct effect on the score for that performance. Although other performances are not judged in the same way (for example, an individual's performance in a football match), how well they complete their tasks is still likely to have an impact on the final score, especially if we consider the team's performance, for example, how well the team completed its tasks (such as attacking and defending).

Components of fitness

The importance of these components will vary depending on the activity. For example, look at Figure 9.6 and 9.7. Would these performers need the same components of fitness in order to be fit enough for their sports?

To improve our health and fitness, we can exercise and improve the components of fitness. Increasing our fitness should have a positive impact on our performance, provided we improve the right components for our activity.

There are eleven components of fitness that you need to know, as shown in Figure 9.8.

Cardiovascular fitness (aerobic endurance)

Cardiovascular fitness is a very important aspect of fitness. If someone has high levels of cardiovascular fitness it means they can work or exercise the entire body for long periods of time. Can you think of any sports performers that would need this component of fitness?

Figure 9.6 Alpine skiing slalom visually impaired event

Figure 9.7 Cycling

The cardiovascular system achieves this by supplying the body with enough oxygen so that it can continue to release energy, provided the intensity of the activity is not too great. For example, marathon runners are able to exercise their bodies for long periods of time (in excess of

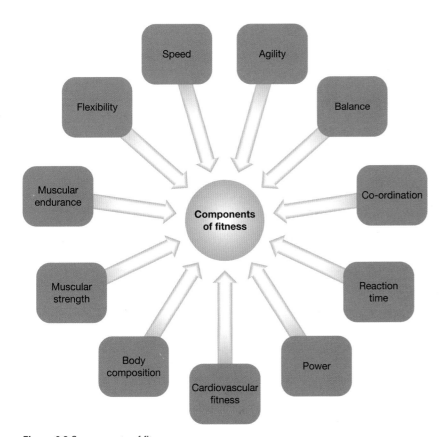

Figure 9.8 Components of fitness

| cardio | and | vascular |

Figure 9.9 Cardiovascular fitness

two hours), but you would not expect a sprinter to be able to sprint for the same amount of time. This is because sprinters' bodies do not have enough time to release energy using oxygen, as they are working anaerobically. This is explained further in Chapter 5.

Cardiovascular fitness is also very important to a healthy lifestyle. The word cardiovascular can be split into two – see Figure 9.9.

Cardiovascular fitness is concerned with the heart, the blood and the blood vessels, see Figures 9.10 and 9.11

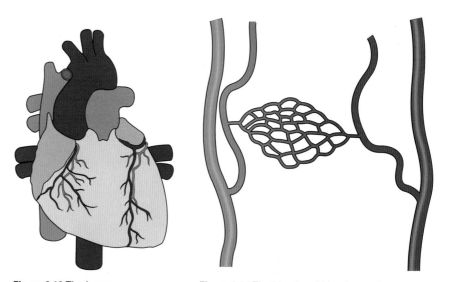

Figure 9.10 The heart   **Figure 9.11** The blood and blood vessels

It is important to health, as there are a number of cardiovascular diseases that could result in death if left unchecked. High blood pressure, heart attacks and strokes are all caused by disorders in the cardiovascular system. Fortunately, a programme of exercise can help maintain cardiovascular fitness.

Strength

This is a very important component of fitness for many different physical activities. It is the amount of force a muscle can exert against a resistance. For example, in cricket, the greater the muscular force (generated by using the strength of their muscles) the batsman uses to hit the ball, the further the ball should go. In gymnastics, gymnasts use muscular strength to support their own body weight in a variety of techniques and balances, for example a handstand or a balance on the rings.

Figure 9.12 Elite gymnast using strength to support body weight on the rings

Muscular endurance

Muscular endurance is the ability to use the voluntary muscles many times without getting tired. Athletes with high levels of muscular endurance can repeatedly use their muscles to continue working throughout their events, allowing them to maintain the quality of their performance. Why would a badminton player need high levels of muscular endurance in his or her arms?

Actions

Make a table and list as many sports as you can think of in the first column. Tick each of the sports that you think requires a high level of muscular endurance.

Write a short statement to explain why you have selected each sport.

Body composition

Body composition is the percentage of body weight that is fat, muscle and bone. This means how much of the body is made up of fat compared with the amount of the body that is made up of lean body mass (bone and muscle). For example, if you weighed 63.5 kg and had 15 per cent body fat, it would mean that your body had 9.5 kg of fat and 54 kg of lean body mass.

Actions

Using Table 9.2 identify the sports activities where performers have the greatest body fat score. Which group has the lowest? Can you draw any conclusions about the relationship between the type of activity and percentage of body fat?

Sport	Male % body fat	Female % body fat
Basketball	6–12%	20–28%
Hockey	8–14%	12–18%
Gymnastics	5–13%	10–16%
Rowing	6–14%	12–19%
Field athletics – jumpers	9–12%	10–18%
Field athletics – throwers	14–20%	20–28%
Triathlon	5–12%	10–15%

Source: adapted from www.brianmac.demon.co.uk/fatcent.htm (October 2015) based on data collected in 1994

Table 9.2 Percentage fat scores in different activities

It is important for all of us to have some body fat in order to allow the body to function properly. The percentage of fat that we have compared with lean body mass will have an impact on our performance in sport. Table 9.2 shows some percentage body fat scores for performers in different activities.

Actions

Identify how each of these five components of fitness (cardiovascular fitness, strength, muscular endurance, body composition and flexibility) are used by the gymnast in Figure 9.12 to ensure they are fit for their activity.

Flexibility

Flexibility is important to all athletes to differing degrees. Flexibility is the range of movement possible at a joint, how far we can stretch or reach.

An increase in flexibility can help prevent muscle injury in some activities where the intensity of work can be explosive, for example in sprinting and football, and is very important in performers in their teens as the body is still growing and developing. Increased flexibility in tennis players will allow for further stretching to reach the ball, but too much flexibility could lead to greater risk of joint injury as the joint becomes less stable. Regular stretching will increase the flexibility of a joint, although the actual shape of the joint (the way the bones fit together) will limit the amount of movement possible (see Chapter 1 for more information).

Check your understanding

4. List five other sports (aside from sprinting and throwing the javelin) where it would be an advantage for the performer if they had high levels of speed. Make sure you select five different activities.

Speed

We all know that speed is to do with how fast we move and we easily accept that speed is important to sprinters so that they can cover the distance of their race quicker than anyone else and win. But speed is equally important to a javelin thrower. Speed in this case refers to how quickly the thrower can move the arm during the throwing action: the faster the arm speed, the further the javelin should go.

Reaction time

This is the time between the presentation of a stimulus and the onset of a movement. This is a very important component in activities where decisions have to be made quickly, for example, when you realise your badminton opponent has just played a disguised shot and you need to move forward to the front of the court to retrieve it, or when the ball hits the top of the net in tennis and bounces off at an unusual angle. The stimulus is the thing you need to respond to, in this example the tennis ball; the onset of movement is when you start to move. What would be the stimulus for a badminton player?

Balance

Balance is described as the ability to retain the body's centre of mass (gravity) above the base of support. Balance can be static (stationary), or dynamic (changing), depending on the situation. Gymnasts obviously use balance to hold themselves still when performing techniques, such as handstands and headstands. This is static balance, but other performers need dynamic balance. For example, for a rugby player swerving through the opposition en route to a try, or resisting a tackle and continuing on their run and a hockey player changing direction at full speed, dynamic balance is critical so they do not fall.

Agility

Agility is the ability to change the position of the body quickly and to control the movement of the whole body. Agility is about changing your direction

Figure 9.13 Maintaining dynamic balance

quickly. A 100m sprinter does not need agility in their event as they run on a straight track. Games players do need agility, as they are constantly changing direction to avoid being tackled by their opposition, or to put themselves in a position to tackle, or to move into a space. Once again, the demands of the activity dictate which components of fitness are important to the performer.

Co-ordination

This refers to the ability to use two or more body parts together. This component of fitness is very important in physical activity. Activities that require the performer to strike an object, for example, volleyball, cricket and squash, require good hand–eye co-ordination. The body needs to be able to move the hand so that it arrives in the correct place to strike the ball and it cannot do this without good co-ordination. It also has to do this in a controlled manner, so that the shot or stroke is played as the player intended.

Other activities, such as football, rugby and Gaelic football, require good foot–eye co-ordination, so that the foot arrives in the correct place to make contact with the ball.

Other examples of co-ordination include the combined use of arms and legs in sprinting to make sure the sprinter reaches the maximum speed, or the discus thrower co-ordinating his move across the circle and the movement of his arm to get the best possible speed, height and angle of release, so that the discus travels further.

Power

Power is the ability to do strength performances quickly. Power is also expressed as an equation: power = strength × speed. To be powerful, then, you need both speed and strength. A gymnast uses power during the tumbling routine, where their movements explode from the floor. A tennis player will use power during the service when the racket arm is brought through quickly and with strength, so that the racket hits the ball with power to make the serve difficult to return.

Figure 9.14 Co-ordinating body movements to get a good throw

Figure 9.15 Components of fitness needed to be successful in sculling

Actions

The performers in Figure 9.15 will rely on a number of components of fitness to be successful in their performance.

List the components they would benefit from and rank them in order in terms of their importance to the activity (with 1 being the most important and 11 being the least important). Justify your rank order.

Actions

Copy and complete Table 9.3 by selecting the important components of fitness for each of the activities listed. Give an example of how the component provides a benefit to the performance.

Hockey	Gymnastics	Marathon
Reaction time – so the player can decide the best direction to avoid an on-coming opponent who is trying to tackle them	Strength – to support their body weight when balancing, e.g. in a handstand	Cardiovascular endurance – so they can maintain a good pace for the full length of the race and get a good time

Table 9.3 Components of fitness and their importance in physical activity and sport

Actions

Think about the activities for which you are being assessed in your practical work. What are the important components of fitness for these activities? How do they help your performance? Do you need to improve any of these? Would it make any difference to your overall performance?

PRACTICE QUESTIONS

1. Define the term health.

2. Which of the following is a definition of performance?
   A The ability to meet the demands of the environment.
   B A state of complete emotional, physical and social well-being and not merely the absence of disease and infirmity.
   C A form of physical activity done to maintain or improve health and/or fitness; it is not competitive sport.
   D How well a task is completed.

3. Explain why a gymnast would need speed during a floor routine.

4. Give an example of the use of reaction time in boxing.

5. Explain one component of fitness that would increase the fitness of the performer in Figure 9.16 for their activity.

Figure 9.16 Which component of fitness would be a benefit to performance in golf?

Summary

- There is a relationship between health, fitness, exercise and performance.
- There are eleven components of fitness.
- Good performance in any physical activity or sport will rely on some components of fitness more than others.

Useful websites

11 components of physical fitness
www.bringithomepersonaltraining.com/components-of-physical-fitness/

Components of physical fitness in action
https://www.youtube.com/watch?v=9pLfcFAYhiw

Performance fitness
www.bbc.co.uk/bitesize/higher/pe/preparation_of_body/performance_fitness/revision/4/

Chapter 10 Physical training – fitness testing and interpretation of results

Learning goals

By the end of this chapter you should be able to:

- give examples of personal readiness questions for a PARQ
- assess personal readiness for activity using a PARQ
- discuss the value of fitness testing
- describe fitness test protocols
- select an appropriate fitness test for a given component of fitness
- use normative data tables to evaluate fitness levels.

Knowledge that you develop through this chapter should also be applied to the personal exercise programme (PEP) that you need to design, carry out and evaluate for the final part of your assessment. More information on this can be found in Chapter 24.

PARQ

Activity as part of a healthy, active lifestyle should be planned in order to be safe and effective. This chapter explains the principles that should be applied before engaging on a planned programme of exercise.

Key word

PARQ – physical activity readiness questionnaire. A series of questions that should be asked before engaging in increased levels of physical activity, to ensure there are not health issues that should be taken into account when planning intensity of exercise

---

Young Person's 'Physical Activity Readiness' Questionnaire

Dear Parent/Guardian,

There are many health benefits to be gained from regular exercise, but it is important to consider the level of health before commencing a physical exercise programme. This questionnaire aims to identify any potential health issues your child may have so that we avoid any risk of injury and can also provide appropriate exercise advice.

Young person's registration information

First Name: .... Surname: ....

Address: ....

....

.... Postcode: ....

Home No: .... Mobile No: ....

Gender: Male/Female (please circle)   Date of Birth: ....

Continued

The following questions relate to the health of the young person. Please read the questions carefully and provide a correct answer by circling Yes or No. Where necessary, please provide details.

			Details
Has a doctor ever diagnosed your child with a heart condition?	Yes	No	
Has your child recently had chest pains during or after exercise?	Yes	No	
Does your child ever feel faint or have spells of severe dizziness:	Yes	No	
Is your child currently receiving treatment or medication for high blood pressure?	Yes	No	
Is your child currently receiving treatment or medication for any other condition?	Yes	No	
Has your child broken any bones in the past six months?	Yes	No	
Does your child suffer from any bone or joint problems which exercise may aggravate?	Yes	No	
Does your child suffer from epilepsy or chronic asthma?	Yes	No	
Is your child diabetic? If yes, is the diabetes Type 1 or Type 2?	Yes	No	
Has your child undergone any recent surgery?	Yes	No	
Is there any other reason which has not been mentioned that may affect your child if they took part in physical activities?	Yes	No	

Figure 10.1 PARQ

Before undertaking increased levels of exercise, individuals should assess their readiness for physical activity. This is normally done through a personal activity readiness questionnaire (PARQ). The first page of an example PARQ is shown in Figure 10.1.

Actions

1. Research and collect copies of existing PARQs from:
   - the internet
   - local sports centres
   - your school.
2. In small groups compare the PARQs.
   - Are there any common questions?
   - What are the questions checking?
   - How would this help to judge an individual's readiness for activity?
3. Individually create your own PARQ based on your research.
4. Work with a partner.
   - Discuss the questions on your PARQ, helping them to complete the PARQ.
   - Discuss the results – are they ready for physical activity?

Having established through a PARQ that it is appropriate to increase activity levels, the next step in a planned programme is to find out current fitness levels so you can plan appropriate workloads. This can be achieved through fitness testing.

Each of the components of fitness identified in Chapter 9 can be 'measured' using specifically designed fitness tests.

Actions

Copy Table 10.1. Without turning back to the previous chapter, add the components of fitness to the first column.

Component of Fitness	Fitness Test to Measure Component of Fitness

Table 10.1 Fitness testing components of fitness

Why fitness test?

Before looking at each fitness test in detail we should first establish why we use fitness testing.

The value of fitness testing

1. Having data about how good (or not) we are can be motivating, encouraging us to do more physical activity to improve the scores or ratings we achieved.
2. Fitness testing provides us with baseline data so we can see:
   a. what our current level of fitness is
   b. what our strengths and areas for improvement are in relation to aspects of fitness
   c. if our fitness 'strengths' match the requirements of our sport
   d. the intensity we should pitch our training at so we work hard enough but not too hard to cause injury
   e. if our training is working.
3. As a result of analysing our fitness test results we can set clear goals or targets for improvement.

The majority of the following fitness tests are general fitness tests for the components of fitness; they are not necessarily sport specific. They are designed to give us an idea of our rating for the component of fitness being tested. When you come to complete fitness testing for your PEP you will be able to use these fitness tests, or any other recognised fitness test that may be more sport specific and therefore more relevant for you to use. For example, the test included in this chapter is for grip strength,

Check your understanding
1. What is a PARQ?

Actions

Work with a partner to produce a list of the top five reasons you think we should fitness test. Compare your ideas with the rest of the group.

Key words

Baseline data (fitness) – initial collection of fitness test data so we can compare fitness levels before and after training

Test protocol – method used to carry out the fitness test

Normative data tables – a table of other people's scores on a fitness test that we can use to judge our fitness levels against

Check your understanding
2. Apart from establishing initial fitness levels, why else would you use fitness tests?

but you may be more interested in leg strength and therefore may use a leg strength test for your PEP, such as a squats test. Whatever tests you use for your PEP, the fitness tests contained in this chapter should be learnt for your written exam.

Fitness tests
Tests to measure cardiovascular fitness
Cooper 12-minute run

Test protocol
- Work in pairs so that one person runs while the other can keep track of distance covered (for example, number of laps).
- Use a 400m track (to make measuring easy) and run around it as many times as possible in 12 minutes. Measure the total distance you cover. (Although the test says this is a run, if you cannot run for 12 minutes you can complete using a mixture of running and walking.)
- Calculate the total distance covered.
- Use normative data tables to get your rating.

An example of a normative data table is shown in Table 10.2. They give us something to compare our fitness tests results against. The data in the tables is based on the scores achieved by large numbers of other people. If a data table doesn't exist for a fitness test you want to conduct for your

MALE RATINGS	AGE		
Rating	13–14	15–16	17–19
Excellent	>2700 m	>2800 m	>3000 m
Above average	2400–2700 m	2500–2800 m	2700–3000 m
Average	2200–2399 m	2300–2499 m	2500–2699 m
Below average	2100–2199 m	2200–2299 m	2300–2499 m
Poor	<2100 m	<2200 m	<2300 m

FEMALE RATINGS	AGE		
Rating	13–14	15–16	17–19
Excellent	>2000 m	>2100 m	>2300 m
Above average	1900–2000 m	2000–2100 m	2100–2300 m
Average	1600–1899 m	1700–1999 m	1800–2099 m
Below average	1500–1599 m	1600–1699 m	1700–1799 m
Poor	<1500 m	<1600 m	<1700 m

Table 10.2 Normative data for the Cooper 12-minute run

PEP, you will need to convince others in your group to also complete the test so you have something to compare your results against.

Normative data tables may vary. Provided you use the same data table to assess your fitness before your exercise programme and after this will not matter. You will not need to learn the values in the normative data tables (these would always be given in a question), but you might need to use them in your exam.

Symbols you will see on data tables: '<' this means less than, so if you are male, between the ages of 15 and 16 and scored <2200 m in the Cooper 12-minute run your rating would be 'poor'.

'>' this means greater than, so if you are female, between the ages of 17 and 19 and scored >2300 m your rating would be 'excellent'.

Cooper 12-minute swim

Test protocol

- Record the length of the pool the test will take place in (for example, 20, 25, 50 m).
- Work in pairs so that one person swims while the other can keep track of distance covered (for example, number of lengths).
- Swim for 12 minutes, using any stroke, resting as needed.
- Calculate the total distance covered.
- Use normative data tables to get your rating.

RATING (13–19)	MALES	FEMALES
Excellent	>732 m	>640 m
Good	640–731 m	549–639 m
Fair	549–639 m	457–548 m
Poor	457–548 m	366–456 m
Very Poor	< 457 m	<366 m

Table 10.3 Normative data for the Cooper 12-minute swim

Harvard step test

Test protocol

- Use a standard gym bench (45 cm).
- Record resting heart rate.
- Step up and down off the bench in time to the metronome/tape for five minutes (once every two seconds).
- One minute after exercise take heart rate for 30 seconds. Record as rate 1.
- Take heart rate again after two minutes, for 30 seconds, and record as rate 2 and finally after 3 minutes for 30 seconds and record as rate 3.
- Calculate your score using the following formula:

  Score = 100 × (300 seconds/2 × (pulse1 + pulse2 + pulse3)

Key words

< – this is the symbol for less than

> – this is the symbol for more than

Check your understanding

3. What rating would a female swimmer achieve if they swam 600 m in the Cooper 12-minute swim test?

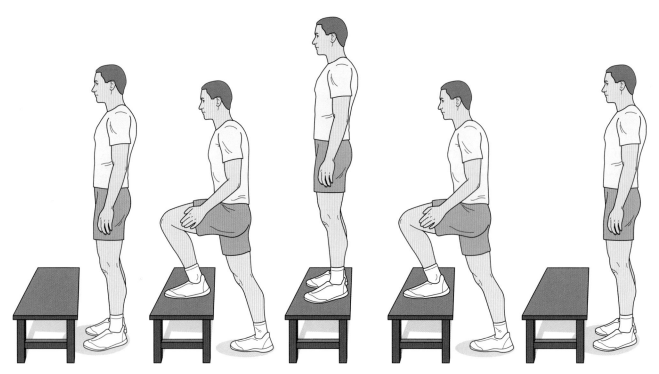

Figure 10.2 Sequence of stepping action in Harvard step test

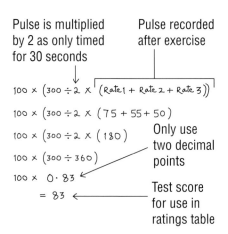

Pulse is multiplied by 2 as only timed for 30 seconds

Pulse recorded after exercise

$$100 \times (300 \div 2 \times (Rate\,1 + Rate\,2 + Rate\,3))$$
$$100 \times (300 \div 2 \times (75 + 55 + 50))$$
$$100 \times (300 \div 2 \times (180))$$
$$100 \times (300 \div 360)$$
$$100 \times 0.83$$
$$= 83$$

Only use two decimal points

Test score for use in ratings table

Once you have calculated your score for the Harvard step test you can use Table 10.4 to determine your rating for this fitness component.

	EXCELLENT	ABOVE AVERAGE	AVERAGE	BELOW AVERAGE	POOR
MALE	>90	80–90	65–79	55–64	<55
FEMALE	>86	76–86	61–75	50 – 60	<50

Table 10.4 Normative data for the Harvard step test
Source: http://www.brianmac.co.uk/havard.htm#ref

Test to measure strength

Grip dynamometer

Test protocol

- Using a hand grip dynamometer (see Figure 10.3), adjust the grip if required.
- With your elbow at your side and your lower arm at right angles to the body, squeeze the dynamometer with maximum effort and hold for five seconds before releasing.
- Read dial for strength measurement. Repeat three times on each hand with a minute's rest between attempts.
- Use your best result from each hand to get your rating from a normative data table.

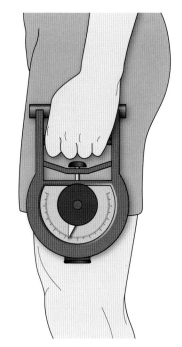

Figure 10.3 Grip dynamometer

RATING (15–19)	MALES (KgW)	FEMALES (KgW)
Excellent	>52	>32
Good	47–51	28–31
Average	44–46	25–27
Below average	39–43	20–24
Poor	<39	<20

Table 10.5 Normative data for the grip dynamometer test

Test to measure muscular endurance

Muscular endurance can be tested through any test that requires the performer to use the same muscle or group of muscles repeatedly.

One-minute sit-up test

Test protocol

- Get someone to help with this test to keep count and to monitor the time allowed.
- Lie on a mat with your knees bent.
- Make sure your feet are flat on the floor (a partner could hold your feet if you wish).
- Cross your arms over your chest.
- Sit up from this position so that your back is at 90 degrees to the floor then return to the floor.
- Record the number of times you can do this in a minute and compare your scores to the data in Table 10.6.

Figure 10.4 Sit-up position

RATING	MALES NUMBER OF REPS	FEMALES NUMBER OF REPS
Excellent	>49	>42
Good	43–48	36–41
Above average	39–42	32–35
Average	35–38	28–31
Below average	31–34	24–27
Poor	<30	<23

Table 10.6 Normative data for the one-minute sit-up test

One-minute press-up test

Test protocol

- Get someone to help with this test to keep count and to monitor the time allowed.
- Lie face down on a mat.
- Place your hands shoulder width apart and extend your arms so they are straight. See Figure 10.5 for position.
- Lower your body until your elbows are bent to 90 degrees. See Figure 10.6 for position.
- Record the number of times you can do this in a minute and compare your scores to the data in Table 10.7.

Table 10.7 Normative data for the one-minute press-up test

RATING	MALES NUMBER OF REPS	FEMALES NUMBER OF REPS
Excellent	>45	>34
Good	35–45	17–34
Average	20–34	6–16
Poor	<20	<5

Test to measure speed

30 m sprint

Test protocol

- Make sure you have someone to tell you when to start and to time your run.
- Start from a stationary position behind the starting line.
- When the signal to go is given, run as fast as possible for 30 m. Do not slow down as you approach the finish.
- Compare your score to the times in Table 10.8.

Figure 10.5 Press-up position (extended arm at elbow)

Figure 10.6 Press-up position (flexed arm at elbow)

RATING	MALES (TIME)	FEMALES (TIME)
Excellent	<4.0	<4.5
Good	4.2–4.0	4.6–4.5
Average	4.4–4.3	4.8–4.7
Fair	4.6–4.5	5.0–4.9
Poor	>4.6	>5.0

Table 10.8 Normative data for the 30 m sprint test

Test to measure power

Vertical jump

Test protocol

- Stand feet together sideways onto the board.
- Place chalk on fingers and mark standing height on jump board (arm extended above head).
- Crouch down and leap up, marking board at top of jump (arms above head).
- Repeat three times.
- Read off distance between two marks and compare with data in Table 10.9.

RATING	MALES (CM)	FEMALES (CM)
Excellent	>60	>55
Good	50–60	45–55
Average	40–49	35–44
Fair	30–39	25–34
Poor	<30	<25

Table 10.9 Normative data for the vertical jump test

Figure 10.7 The vertical jump would be an appropriate test for basketball players.

Test to measure agility

Illinois agility run

Test protocol

- Make sure you have someone to tell you when to start and to time your run.
- Set up the test as shown in Figure 10.8 on a flat, dry non-slip surface.
- Start by lying on your front, so that your head is just behind the start line.
- On 'go' run the course as quickly as possible.
- Compare your score to the times in Table 10.10.

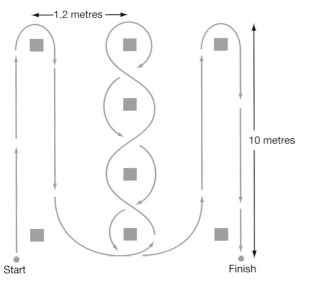

Figure 10.8 Illinois agility run test

Check your understanding

4. Which would be a better time in the 30 m sprint test – <4.5 seconds or >4.5 seconds?

RATING	MALES (SECONDS)	FEMALES (SECONDS)
Excellent	<15.2	<17.0
Good	16.1–15.2	19.9–17.0
Average	18.1–16.2	21.7–18.0
Fair	19.3–18.2	23.0–21.8
Poor	>19.3	>23.0

Table 10.10 Normative data for the Illinois agility run test

Test to measure flexibility

Sit and reach

Test protocol

- Remove your shoes.
- Using a sit and reach box, sit on the floor with your legs out straight and feet flat against the box.
- Keeping your legs straight, bend forward and push the ruler on the top of the box as far away from you as possible.
- The ruler should be placed at 0 cm on the scale on the box; this should be at the front edge of the box.
- Record your score and compare it to the distances in Table 10.11.

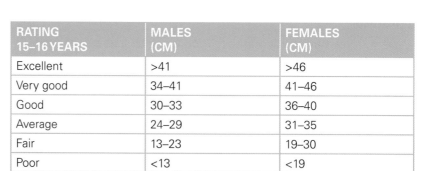

Figure 10.9 Sit and reach test

RATING 15–16 YEARS	MALES (CM)	FEMALES (CM)
Excellent	>41	>46
Very good	34–41	41–46
Good	30–33	36–40
Average	24–29	31–35
Fair	13–23	19–30
Poor	<13	<19

Table 10.11 Normative data for the sit and reach test

Check your understanding

5. What part of the body's flexibility does the sit and reach test?

Actions

1. Go back to Table 10.1 and add the appropriate name of the fitness test for each of the listed components of fitness. Where you have gaps, use the internet to research sport specific tests that relate to the sport you will be basing your PEP on.
2. Add a third column to the table, this time giving an example of a sport that could use the fitness test to measure a performer's fitness for that activity. For example, basketball and the vertical jump test. Justify the reasons for your selections.

6. Complete Table 10.12 by naming the fitness test each image represents and the component of fitness it is used to measure.

Image	Name of test	Component measured

Table 10.12 Identifying fitness tests

Actions

Look at the fitness test ratings in Table 10.13.

1. If these were the test results for a 1500 m runner what component(s) of fitness would you suggest they worked on and why?
2. What area of fitness would you test in addition to the tests listed here?

Fitness Test	Rating
Cooper 12-minute run	Above average
Grip dynamometer	Average
Sit and reach	Average
Speed	Fair
Vertical jump	Poor

Table 10.13 Using fitness test ratings

Actions

Select the most appropriate fitness tests for your PEP and with the help of your teacher complete the fitness tests, recording your scores. Use the data tables provided and work out your ratings. Are you fit for your sport?

PRACTICE QUESTIONS

1. A basketball coach is given a new team to coach. Explain how the coach could use fitness testing to establish who should play in the first game.
2. Describe the test protocol for the Cooper 12-minute run.
3. Explain the advantage of the Cooper 12-minute test being a running or swimming test.
4. Identify the fitness test a player would use if they wanted to measure the muscular endurance of the muscles in their upper body.
5. Evaluate whether the 30 m sprint would be a suitable test for a 100 m sprinter.

Study hints

Think about the question context; for example, in question 1 in the practice box there are lots of reasons to use fitness testing but this question wants you to focus on using fitness tests to pick a team.

Summary

- a PARQ is used to assess personal readiness for physical activity.
- fitness testing gives baseline data.
- fitness test protocols tell us how to carry out fitness tests.
- each fitness test is designed to measure a given component of fitness.
- normative data tables are used to evaluate fitness levels.

Useful websites
Fitness testing with England Rugby
https://www.youtube.com/watch?v=o0z6qaUbJbg

Fitness tests section
www.sport-fitness-advisor.com/fitnesstests.html

Chapter 11 Physical training – the principles of training and their application

Learning goals

By the end of this chapter you should be able to:

- identify the principles of training
- describe the principles of training
- explain how to apply the principles of training when planning training.

Key word

Principles of training – a set of ideas/values that should be followed in order to make training effective

You need to know about the principles of training because correct application of them within your PEP should lead to an improvement in aspects of your fitness. In other words, they are 'rules' which, if followed, allow your training to be more effective. This should have a positive impact on your performance in whichever sporting activity you participate and on your health, helping you lead an active and healthy lifestyle.

Figure 11.1 shows the principles of training that you are required to know for the Edexcel GCSE PE specification.

A useful way to help you remember the different principles of training is to create a mnemonic, a word where each letter of the word represents one of the principles of training. For example, RIPS could be used to remember some of the principles. Have a look at Figure 11.1; what principles would you remember by linking to RIPS?

Unfortunately, RIPS does not cover all of the principles you need to know. The other letters involved are 'F', 'T' and 'O'.

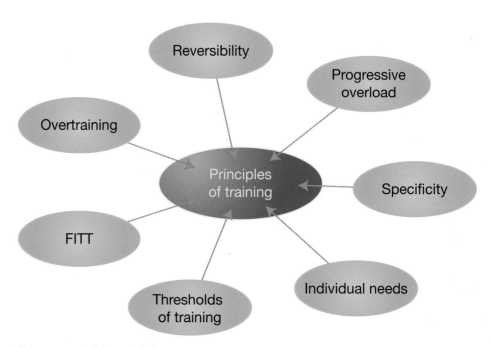

Figure 11.1 Principles of training

Remembering the names of the principles is a good start, but you will also be expected to describe them, or recognise them from their description or definition and show how you might apply them in a personal exercise programme (PEP) to improve aspects of fitness.

Although you will not need to remember exact definitions of these terms for your assessment, they are a good way of demonstrating the meaning of the principle.

Specificity

This principle of training is stating that you cannot just do any type of training, but that you must match your training to the needs of your sport.

Progressive overload

What training do you currently do? If you wanted to apply the principle of progressive overload, what would you have to do to the amount of training you currently do? Give a specific example.

There are three critical parts to this training principle:

- Gradually increase
- the amount of work you normally do
- without the potential for injury.

In your exam you might be asked to give an example of progressive overload. If you remember these three parts to the principle it should be easy to answer this sort of question. For example, if you currently train twice a week, you would be overloading by training three times a week (this is a gradual increase, from two to three and therefore should not result in injury). The reason for overloading the body is that by making it work harder it has to adapt to the new work rate, therefore making you 'fitter'.

These adaptations are dealt with later in the book in Chapter 12, but the way in which the body adapts makes it easier for the sports performer to perform well.

For example, a sprinter should run faster once their body has adapted to extra physical work, because they are becoming more muscular and can therefore generate more power to decrease their time.

Overtraining

It is vital that you plan adequate rest in any training programme to allow your body to recover from the physical work you are making it do. Without appropriate rest the body does not have time to:

- replenish energy stores
- repair damage to muscle tissue
- allow adaptations to muscles to take place
- relax and de-stress
- reduce feelings of physical fatigue.

But how do you know if you are doing too much? A simple checklist like the one following could be used. If you total less than 20 points you're probably not ready for an intensive workout!

Rate each statement on a 1–5 scale as follows: 1 = strongly disagree; 2 = disagree; 3 = neutral; 4 = agree; 5 = strongly agree.

Actions

Working with a partner, can you come up with a meaningful word to help you remember the principles of training?

Would any of these work for you?

SPORT FI

SPORT IF

FIRST PO

Key words

Specificity – matching training to the requirements of an activity or a position within an activity

Progressive overload – to gradually increase the amount of work done so that fitness gains occur, but without potential for injury

Overtraining – a decrease in performance due to insufficient rest and recovery from training sessions

Check your understanding

1. Why do we need both parts of the principle of progressive overload and not just overload?

Source: http://www.pponline.co.uk/encyc/0685.htm October 2015

1. I slept really well last night.
2. I am looking forward to today's workout.
3. I am optimistic about my future performance(s).
4. I feel vigorous and energetic.
5. My appetite is great.
6. I have very little muscle soreness.

Lack of rest and recovery can lead to overtraining. This is not helpful as it can lead to you feeling depressed and lethargic, can increase the chance of injury and generally can lead to a drop in performance – not the desired effect! Recovery can be short-term or long-term. Short-term recovery could be a cool-down at the end of a session or working at a lower intensity in the next couple of training sessions, so that over the training week there is a balance and opportunity for recovery. Long-term recovery is the rest/recovery periods built into a seasonal training programme to make sure the performer has adequate rest, so they can perform at their best at the right time for their sporting year.

Reversibility

You would not willingly apply this principle to your training. It describes what happens to your levels of fitness if you have a break in your training because of an injury, a holiday, because it is the end of the season or because you do not want to train any more. In the same way that your body adapts to an increased level of physical work, it will readapt to a lower level of physical work so you will in effect lose fitness.

Thresholds of training

It is important to train at the correct intensity for your activity (aerobic or anaerobic) and for yourself (considering your age and current level of fitness). The basic Karvonen formula (Max HR – age) should be used to calculate training thresholds. It is suggested that the average performer should train:

- Aerobically at 60–80 per cent of their maximum heart rate, although elite performers will often train outside of this range.
- Anaerobically at 80–90 per cent of their maximum heart rate.

The actual percentage that is used to represent maximum and minimum training thresholds will vary depending on the level of the performer and what they are trying to achieve, but the principle explained below remains the same. To help us achieve the correct training intensity we use target training zones.

The top line on the graph in Figure 11.2 represents the maximum heart rate (beats per minute – bpm) values for the age groups specified (15, 20, 25, 30). This value is calculated by using the Karvonen formula by taking the performer's age from the base rate of 220 bpm. The middle line represents the maximum aerobic training threshold (80 per cent of maximum heart rate) and the lower line represents the minimum aerobic training threshold (60 per cent of maximum heart rate). The area between the minimum and maximum training thresholds is called the target zone. This is the area that you should try to work within so that your body is working hard enough to cause aerobic adaptations, but not so hard that the training has a negative effect.

Check your understanding

2. How would you ensure you did not overtrain?

3. If your body becomes fitter as a result of extra physical work in training, what is likely to happen to your level of fitness if you do less physical work?

Key words

Reversibility – the loss of training adaptations due to a reduction in training levels

Training thresholds – the upper and lower limits of target zones. Target zones are the heart rate ranges an individual should work within to achieve aerobic or anaerobic gains

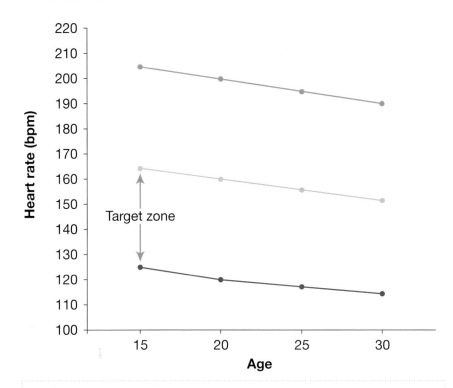

Figure 11.2 Aerobic training threshold

Actions

Table 11.1 shows the actual heart rate values used to produce the graph in Figure 11.2. If maximum heart rate is calculated by subtracting the performer's age from 220, what are the heart rate values for performers aged 45 and 50 and their aerobic target zones? Copy and complete Table 11.1.

	15	20	25	30	35	40	45	50
Maximum heart rate (MHR)	205	200	195	190	185	180		
80% MHR	164	160	156	152	148	144		
60% MHR	123	120	117	114	111	108		

Table 11.1 Calculating aerobic threshold of training

FITT

The FITT principle is four principles of training rolled into one. Each letter represents a part of this principle. The FITT principle is used to increase the amount of physical work the body does, in other words how you achieve overload. The first three letters in the principle are ways of achieving overload and the fourth letter is a reminder that the overload needs to be specific to the activity for which you are training. According to this principle, you work harder than before but within your target zone, gradually increasing the amount of work you do.

Individual needs

This principle of training is similar to the principle of specificity. The difference is that this principle considers the needs of the individual rather than the needs of the sporting activity. In other words, according to the principle of specificity, two footballers could do the same training programme. (Consider Wayne Rooney and Danny Welbeck, or any other

Check your understanding

4. What happens to the aerobic target zone as the performer gets older?

Key words

FITT – is made up of four sub-principles: frequency, intensity, time and type

Individual differences/needs – matching training to the requirements of an individual

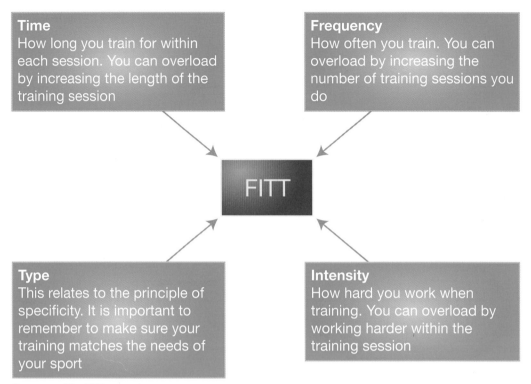

Figure 11.3 The FITT principle

Actions

Explain how age, sex, sporting experience, weight, height and current level of fitness could make a difference to the training programme followed.

two performers. Would you give them the same training programme?) By adding the principle of individual needs we should formulate a much better PEP, as the training will also consider the performer. Factors such as age, sex, sporting experience, weight, height, current level of fitness should all make a difference to the type of training programme followed. If you consider these things when forming your own PEP, then you are applying the principle of individual needs.

Actions

Consider the pairs of performers in Table 11.2. Under the 'rule' of the principle of individual needs and/or specificity, decide whether any of these performers could use the same training programme. Copy and complete this table and justify your answer.

PAIRS OF ATHLETES		SAME PEP YES/NO?
Sprinter	Marathon runner	
Netball player	Squash player	
Dancer	Swimmer	
Tennis player	Table tennis player	
Footballer 1	Footballer 2	

Table 11.2

Actions

1. Create a list of your fitness strengths and areas for improvement (based on your fitness test results).

Using this list:

(a) List the components of fitness you need to improve.

(b) Explain how you would use the principles of training to improve these components of fitness.

2. Copy Table 11.3 and reorganise the statements/terms to give the correct order of the stages you should go through in order to achieve a planned and effective increase in activity as part of a healthy, active lifestyle.

Incorrect order	Correct order
Carry out planned activity	
Complete fitness tests	
Check targets set are SMART targets	
Complete a PARQ	
Re-test fitness levels	
Identify targets	
Re-evaluate fitness plan	
Apply the principles of training to develop an appropriate fitness plan	

Table 11.3

Key words

SMART targets – specific, measureable, achievable, realistic, time-bound (see Chapter 18 for more details)

Training methods

We use training methods to make sure that we tailor our training so it is effective in helping us meet our training targets and goals. Before making your final choice of training method you need to consider:

- the fitness/sport requirements
- facilities available
- your current level of fitness.

Therefore, before preparing your PEP you will need to look at the demands of your sport carefully to see which of the components of fitness are most important. Once you have a clear idea about which aspect of fitness you need to improve, you need to choose a method of training that will bring about those improvements. You also need to consider the access you have to relevant facilities. If you can't get to a gym to use weight machines, for example, you will need to find another way to improve your strength.

Once you have decided on the training method, you will then need to consider the principles of training so that you work at the correct intensity given your current fitness and what you want to achieve. If your sporting activity or your role within it is mainly aerobic or anaerobic or a combination of both, the intensity at which you will have to work should make a difference to the training method you

Check your understanding

5. What principles of training are represented by the words SPORT IF?

select. Some training methods have breaks built in them, whereas others are continuous. Why do you think you might need a break in your training session? How hard would you be working? Is this likely to be aerobic or anaerobic work?

There are several different types of training methods. For this course you need to be able to describe the following methods and give examples of when they would be used:

- continuous training
- Fartlek training
- circuit training
- interval training
- plyometrics
- weight/resistance training.

In addition to these training methods you also need to be familiar with different types of fitness classes that are designed to improve specific components of fitness (body pump, aerobics, Pilates, yoga, spinning).

Continuous training

This develops cardiovascular fitness and muscular endurance. The training is called continuous because you do not rest; it is known as steady state training as you maintain the same intensity of work for at least 30 minutes. It is an aerobic activity that uses large muscle groups; activities include cycling, jogging and step aerobics. Continuous training requires the performer to work between 60 and 80 per cent of their training threshold (see thresholds of training earlier in the chapter), for a minimum of 30 minutes five times a week to have a positive effect on cardiovascular fitness and muscular endurance.

Key words

Continuous training – working at a moderate, steady pace for a minimum of 30 minutes

Fartlek training – training that involves a change in pace or intensity and varied terrains

ADVANTAGES	DISADVANTAGES
No need for specialist equipment or resources as can run locally	It can become boring due to no variation in pace or activity
Easy method of training to organise	Can lead to injury if road running due to impact of running on hard surface
Can run independently or at running clubs	Due to the intensity of the exercise, it only improves aerobic endurance

Table 11.4 Advantages and disadvantages of continuous training

Fartlek training

This is another form of continuous training. It involves running at different paces and over different terrains. For example, rather than road running at a constant pace, you might increase your speed for 50 m and then jog until you have sufficiently recovered before sprinting again. You could run 'off road' through woodland, changing your pace as you go up and down hill. It is a very good training method for games players as it can be tailored to match the demands of the game, for example, mixing spells of relative inactivity (jogging) with intense activity (sprinting). This training method is used to increase cardiovascular fitness.

ADVANTAGES	DISADVANTAGES
More interesting than steady state continuous running due to variation in pace and terrain	Easy to reduce intensity too much if feeling tired/unmotivated
Can be tailored to sport, e.g. games play involves variation in pace	Need high levels of motivation (as easy to reduce intensity)
Not reliant on expensive equipment	Need to consider safety when planning route if unpopulated area or heavy traffic

Table 11.5 Advantages and disadvantages of Fartlek training

Circuit training

The principles of circuit training are as follows:

1. A number of different exercises are carried out at 'stations'.

2. Each exercise should be carefully selected to make sure that it is relevant to the aim or purpose of the sports performer's PEP. For example, if the performer were a games player and they wanted to improve their muscular endurance, they would include exercises that related to their sport and this area of fitness.

3. The stations are normally positioned in a circular order and are completed one after the other.

4. Care has to be taken to organise the circuit so that different muscle groups are used from one station to the next (to allow the muscles to recover between stations).

5. The performer will work on the station for a set number of repetitions or for a set time before moving on to the next station.

6. You can vary how hard a performer works by adjusting:
   - the length of time on each station/number of repetitions at each station
   - the number of times the performer must complete the circuit within one training session
   - the number of times the performer must complete the circuit training session per week
   - the amount of recovery time you allow between each station/ complete circuit.

Circuit training can be used to improve any component of fitness (including skill aspects related to a specific sporting activity), as the exercises and the order in which they are completed can be adapted to suit many needs. For example, as a form of continuous exercise, circuit training can improve cardiovascular fitness. By working on specific groups of muscles at several stations, it can also increase muscular endurance. Strength could also be worked on by including weight bearing exercises (such as press-ups, triceps dips and bench presses using a bench to add resistance) and skills such as passing, shooting and dribbling can be included to improve relevant skill-related aspects of fitness, such as agility and coordination.

Key word

Circuit training – a number of different exercises at stations; rotate from one exercise to the next

Actions

Figures 11.4 and 11.5 show two different facilities where circuit training can take place. Figure 11.4 will be used for a skills circuit and Figure 11.5 for a fitness circuit.

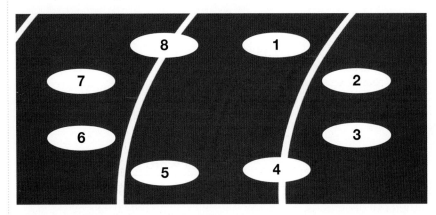

Figure 11.4 Skills circuit

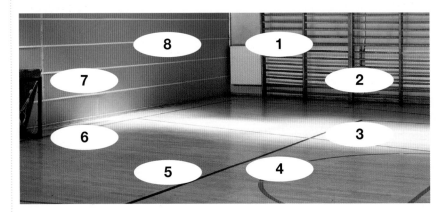

Figure 11.5 Fitness circuit

Each station from the circuit is represented by a number. Choose appropriate activities from Table 11.6 to replace the numbers for each circuit. Make sure you consider the order in which the activities are placed. Copy Table 11.6 and add a further two activities to complete the circuits.

Straight dribble	Press-up	Skipping
Chest pass (against the wall)	Sit-up	Triceps dip
Zigzag dribble	Shuttle run	Bench astride
Shooting		

Table 11.6 Activities of circuit training

ADVANTAGES	DISADVANTAGES
Can use minimal equipment, e.g. benches, cones, skipping rope	Can use extensive equipment if skills circuit
Can improve skill and fitness if appropriate exercise stations selected	Can take time to organise in terms of setting up equipment
Can maintain interest due to different activities	Although can involve skill practice, doesn't give long at station to improve the skill

Table 11.7 Advantages and disadvantages of circuit training

Interval training

Interval training is a form of intermittent training. Breaks are built into the training session in order to allow the performer to recover so that they can continue to work at high levels of intensity. The 'interval' is the period when they reduce the amount of work they are doing to allow recovery. Due to the use of intervals, this type of training is normally considered for high-intensity work.

Sprinters, swimmers and cyclists typically use this type of training, although it can be adapted to suit almost any activity by altering the duration of the work interval, how hard the performer works in the work interval, the number of repetitions within a set, the number of sets, the length of the rest interval and the type of activity carried out during the rest.

Figure 11.6 gives an example of an interval training session.

Key word

Interval training – a form of intermittent training where breaks are built into the training session so that the performer can recover before working again. This training method allows the performer to work at higher intensities

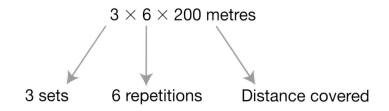

3 × 6 × 200 metres

3 sets   6 repetitions   Distance covered

W:R 1:½

Amount of time working compared with recovery period. In this example the recovery is half as long as the time spent working

Figure 11.6 Interval training

ADVANTAGES	DISADVANTAGES
No specialist equipment required	May be demotivating due to repetition of sets
Clear structure to training, so can adapt to aerobic or anaerobic work	Need to carefully plan training intensities to ensure appropriate gains

Table 11.8 Advantages and disadvantages of interval training

Actions

Would the following interval training sessions be for a performer preparing for an aerobic or an anaerobic activity? W:R indicates the work recovery ratio – how much time spent working compared to resting or recovering.

- 5 × 10 × 50 metres W:R 1:3 Aerobic/anaerobic?
- 5 × 1 × 3000 metres W:R 1:1/2 Aerobic/anaerobic?

Interval training can be used to improve speed or cardiovascular endurance. It will depend on the nature of the work intervals and recovery periods.

Plyometric training

Plyometrics can involve skipping, jumping, bounding, hopping. It can involve the use of boxes or benches to allow jumping from one level to another. In plyometrics, the muscles are worked quickly. The muscles are lengthened as the body lands (for example, as it drops from a jump) and then immediately shortened (for example, as the body takes off again for the next jump) repeatedly. The muscles have to work very hard, exerting maximum force. For an example see Figure 11.7.

Key word

Plyometric training – a form of intermittent training that develops power and strength

Figure 11.7 Plyometric training can involve 'box jumps'

The type of plyometric exercise you choose will vary depending on:

- the area of the body you wish to train
- your current level of fitness.

Bounding and hurdling can be used for the lower body and can be adapted to ensure the correct intensity, for example, standing jumps such as tuck jumps will be low intensity compared to multiple jumps, for example, bunny hops or two-footed jumps over low hurdles, and these will be a lower intensity than depth jumping, which involves dropping down off and immediately jumping up onto a box.

The upper body can be trained using explosive press ups where the performer pushes up off of the floor and claps before lowering the body again. Medicine balls can be used as shown in Figure 11.8 where the performer catches the ball and immediately throws it back.

Figure 11.8 The boxer Amir Khan training with a medicine ball

ADVANTAGES	DISADVANTAGES
Can be carried out with minimal equipment	Can become injured if intensity is too great

Table 11.9 Advantages and disadvantages of plyometric training

Weight/resistance training

Resistance training can involve any aid that increases the work the body has to do. Weight training is one way of doing this. Other types of resistance training include use of resistance bands (see Figure 11.9) or less conventional weights (see Figure 11.10).

Weight training is a form of strength training. You can use free weights (weights that are not attached to machines, such as dumb bells) or weights that are part of a gym machine. You can train to improve muscular strength or muscular endurance. If you chose to increase

Key words

Resistance training – a training method where the performer has to manage an additional weight or resistance when carrying out the exercise; used to increase strength, power or speed

Weight training – is a form of resistance training carried out to improve strength or muscular endurance

Figure 11.9 The England rugby team using resistance bands in training

muscular endurance you would need to lift the weights repeatedly for a number of repetitions and a number of sets. The general standard is 12–20 repetitions per set, for three sets. The weight you use should be light enough to allow you to complete the sets. Strength training, however, requires fewer repetitions and sets but heavier weights. Performers requiring power (such as sprinters and field athletes competing in throwing events) would design their weight training so that they increased their strength, whereas performers who rely heavily on muscular endurance (such as middle to long-distance runners and racket players) would design their programme to increase their muscular endurance.

Figure 11.10 The French rugby team increase the resistance when running in training by dragging heavy weights

ADVANTAGES	DISADVANTAGES
Exercises can target the specific muscles that require additional strength	Can become injured if intensity is too great
Depending on the type of training, can be done with minimal equipment, e.g. body weight or resistance bands	Need to ensure correct technique to prevent injury and to train correct muscles

Table 11.10 Advantages and disadvantages of weight/resistance training

Fitness classes

Fitness classes are often designed to train a specific component of fitness. From time to time a new 'fad' or 'craze' will hit the fitness industry with a specific type of fitness class that appeals to a large number of the population. Some of these classes come and go but others have proved very effective in increasing fitness and motivating people to train. Most classes will run for 60 minutes. The types of fitness classes you should be familiar with are:

- body pump
- aerobics
- Pilates
- yoga
- spinning.

Look at Table 11.11 for a summary of these fitness classes.

Figure 11.11 Weight training can involve free weights or weight machines

FITNESS CLASS	WHAT THE CLASS LOOKS LIKE	WHAT THE CLASS INVOLVES
Body pump		Complete body work out using weights to increase strength or muscular endurance
Aerobics		Complete body work out normally to music – there are many variations to this class including water aerobics (in a swimming pool) and step aerobics (using a step to increase intensity). Focus is on improving cardiovascular fitness
Pilates		Focuses on strength, balance and flexibility. Exercises are carried out on a mat possibly with some form of resistance, e.g. resistance band. Focus is on the muscles in the centre of the body (the core) and movement flows from here to the muscles of the legs and arms
Yoga		Requires minimal equipment, involves static poses that are designed to improve strength, balance and flexibility
Spinning		Indoor cycling workout, normally to music. The instructor will guide participants through a change in intensity by motivating them to pedal harder to increase intensity or slower for recovery before the next increase in intensity. Focuses on cardiovascular fitness and muscular endurance

Table 11.11 Fitness classes

Actions

Consider the training methods covered in this chapter. Which training method would be most appropriate to you given your activity, your role within it, your current level of fitness and the resources available to you?

Actions

Match the images in Figure 11.12 to the training methods or fitness classes discussed.

Actions

Match the type of training that could be carried out to the locations in Figure 11.13.

Actions

Match the performers in Figure 11.14 to the most relevant training method.

Figure 11.12 Which type of training or fitness class is represented in each image?

Figure 11.13 Matching a location to its method of training

Figure 11.14 Matching the performers to the most relevant training method

Actions

Copy the tables below. Tick each training method in Table 11.12 and each fitness class in Table 11.13 that you could use to improve each of the components of fitness listed.

	Continuous	Fartlek	Circuit	Interval	Weight/ resistance	Plyometrics
Flexibility						
Muscular endurance						
Cardiovascular fitness						
Body composition						
Strength						
Power						
Agility						
Speed						

Table 11.12 Training methods for specific components of fitness

	Body pump	Aerobics	Pilates	Yoga	Spinning
Flexibility					
Muscular endurance					
Cardiovascular fitness					
Body composition					
Strength					
Power					
Agility					
Speed					

Table 11.13 Fitness classes for specific components of fitness

Key word

PEP – personal exercise programme. You will need to plan, analyse and evaluate a PEP as part of your assessment

Applying your knowledge to plan a PEP

More information on your practical and PEP can be found in Chapter 24.

You should now have the basic knowledge required to start planning your PEP. You should plan a PEP as part of your assessment for GCSE PE. If your PEP is going to be effective in improving aspects of your fitness, it needs to be well thought out and continually evaluated to check you are doing the right things.

Development of a PEP should go through the following stages:

Planning

1. Check you can increase your activity level safely by completing a PARQ and then reviewing your answers.
2. Identify your goals (what activity do you want to get fit for?).
3. Find out how fit you currently are (carry out some fitness tests).

4. Identify your strengths and weaknesses (analyse your fitness test results).

5. Select the areas of fitness you need to work on (based on your goals and current weaknesses) and set SMART targets.

6. Choose a training method to suit your goal (for example, continuous training to improve cardiovascular endurance).

7. Decide on activities and workload to suit your training method, your current fitness and your goals.

8. Decide on the structure of the exercise session (warm-up, main activity, cool-down).

Performing

Carry out the PEP sessions, collecting data before, during and after the session relating to your fitness or even your performance in the activity you are trying to get fit for.

Make sure you apply the principles of training:

- How you can apply progressive overload.
- At what rate you should apply the overload.
- Monitor your use of target zones to set training levels.
- Consider the possible use of recovery rates to monitor progress.

Evaluating

1. Assess the session (could be via re-test).

2. Plan the next session (change workload, change activities as appropriate).

3. Final testing.

4. Final evaluation (did you achieve your goals? Were the principles of training appropriately applied and was the method of training suitable?).

5. Recommendations for future training (where do you go from here? How would you adapt your training to continue to improve?).

PRACTICE QUESTIONS

1. Which of the examples in Table 11.14 demonstrate the principle of progressive overload?

Example	Progression	Accurate application of progressive overload Yes/no
Train twice a week	Train five times a week	
Work for 30 minutes	Work for 31 minutes	
Complete 25 repetitions	Complete 30 repetitions	
Lift 5 kg	Lift 4 kg	
Work at 70% of my maximum heart rate	Work at 75% of my maximum heart rate	

Table 11.14

PRACTICE QUESTIONS

2. Which principles of training are being referred to in this extract?

Your training is different from your friends', some of whom play different sports. This week you trained for an extra session, although last week you made one of the sessions longer than usual. You think that you might work harder within the session next week, but you have said that you will be careful not to do too much because you do not wish to miss any training sessions through injury, as this could lead to a drop in fitness.

3. Using the Karvonen formula, calculate and plot the anaerobic training thresholds for a 15- and 30- year-old man on the graph in Figure 11.15.

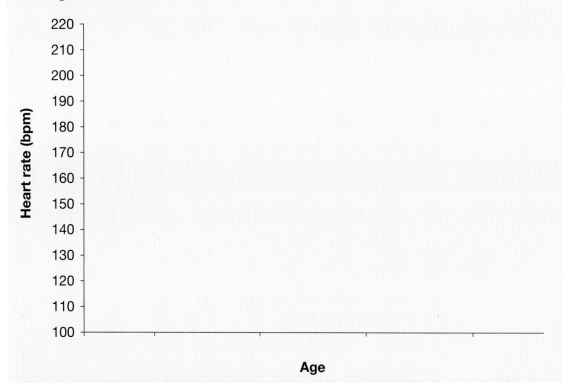

Figure 11.15 Anaerobic training threshold

4. Explain how a badminton coach could use circuit training to improve the skill and fitness of his group of players.

5. Explain why a games player should consider Fartlek training rather than continuous training as their preferred training method.

Study hints
Make sure you read questions carefully and take note of key words. Note the term anaerobic in question 3 above, for example; make sure you get the right percentage of maximum heart rate for the anaerobic threshold.

Summary

- There are seven principles of training.
- The principles of training should be applied to any training programme to increase its effectiveness.
- Fitness is improved by applying the principles of training to a training method.
- Different training methods should be used to improve different components of fitness.
- Different fitness classes are designed to improve specific components of fitness.

Useful websites

Training strategies – principles of training
https://www.youtube.com/watch?v=xyw-Llv4mxQ

Principles and methods of training
http://www.bbc.co.uk/education/guides/z2b9q6f/revision/2

Chapter 12 Physical training – the long term training effects of exercise

Learning goals

By the end of this chapter you should be able to:

- explain the long-term training effects and benefits of exercise on the musculo-skeletal system
- explain the long-term training effects and benefits of exercise on the cardio-respiratory system.

Key word

Long-term training effect – an adaptation to the body that takes place over a long period of time due to regular training

The previous chapters have explored how to increase fitness. But why do athletes want to increase fitness? How does the body adapt to allow the fitter athlete to perform better? This chapter reviews some of the adaptations that occur as a result of training and the benefits this can bring. If you need to refresh your memory about the body systems, go back over Chapters 1 to 4 before continuing with this chapter.

Long-term training effects

If you continue to exercise on a regular basis, following the principles of training, your body will start to adapt to its increased workload, so that in effect the work becomes easier for the body to do (in other words, you become fitter). These adaptations are what you should refer to if asked about the long-term training effects of regular training. For example, if the heart has been working harder on a regular basis it becomes used to this, and over time increases its strength so that it is easier for it to pump a larger amount of blood out of the heart per beat. When this happens we say that the performer has an increased stroke volume, (see Chapter 3). This is an effect of long-term training. The benefit of this training effect is the performer will have a larger stroke volume even when they are at rest and as a result the performer's heart rate at rest will be lower, giving them a greater heart rate range to increase blood flow during exercise.

Check your understanding

1. What causes a long-term training effect?

Long-term benefits of exercise

Changes to the body as a result of regular exercise can also bring about long-term health benefits. For example, exercise can bring about a drop in resting blood pressure. High blood pressure is a common health risk as people grow older. If blood pressure is too high, it can lead to coronary heart failure or a stroke (as the blood is not able to circulate through the blood vessels properly). Therefore, a long-term benefit of exercise is that blood pressure can be reduced, reducing some of the risk factors that cause coronary heart disease and strokes.

When asked a question on this aspect of the course, make sure you double-check whether you are being asked about:

- the short-term effects of exercise
- the long-term effects of regular training, or
- the long-term benefits of exercise.

Obviously, these three areas are linked. We experience the short-term effects of exercise, which if brought into play on a regular basis (through regular exercise) become permanent adaptations (while the level of activity is maintained). These adaptations then bring health benefits. A summary of the long-term training effects and their benefits is given below (the short-term effects of exercise are detailed in Chapter 6).

Long-term training effects and benefits of exercise on the musculo-skeletal system

Muscular system

The type of training you do, aerobic training or anaerobic, will determine the type of training effects you can expect as the body has to adapt to suit the work you are doing. This is why the principles of training, in this case specificity and progressive overload, are so important – if you train in the wrong way for your sport you will not get the adaptations you are looking for.

These are the adaptations you should refer to if asked about the effects of regular training on the muscular system:

Aerobic training adaptations

- Increased size of skeletal muscle through hypertrophy of slow twitch muscle fibres.
- Increased size of mitochondria.
- Increased number of mitochondria.
- Increase in store of energy source in the muscle for aerobic energy production.
- Increased myoglobin content in the muscle (equivalent to an oxygen 'store' in the muscle).

> **Check your understanding**
> 2. Give an example of a long-term benefit of exercise.

Key words

Hypertrophy – an increase in size of muscle fibres

Aerobic training – continuous training at moderate intensity using oxygen for energy production

Figure 12.1 Adaptations to Mo Farah's muscular system due to aerobic training gives him the advantage required to win the race

Key words

Mitochondria – found in the muscles, they are the site of aerobic respiration

Site of aerobic respiration – place in the muscles where oxygen is used to produce energy

Anaerobic training – repeated periods of intense work followed by recovery within the training session; energy production is without oxygen during the intense periods of work

Mitochondria are the site of aerobic respiration. This means they are the place where oxygen is used in energy production within the muscle. They provide the necessary energy for the muscles to contract so they can carry out physical work.

With an increased size and number of mitochondria it is possible to generate:

- aerobic energy more rapidly
- more aerobic energy.

The increase in the stores of the energy sources used in aerobic respiration in the muscle also means that the muscles can produce greater amounts of energy provided there is sufficient oxygen available. This is helped by having greater stores of myoglobin in the muscle, acting as oxygen stores, so oxygen is already present in the muscle for aerobic energy production.

Anaerobic training adaptations

- Increased strength of ligaments.
- Increased strength of tendons.
- Increase in store of energy source in the muscle for anaerobic energy production.
- Increased tolerance to lactic acid.
- Increased strength of skeletal muscle through hypertrophy of fast twitch muscle fibres.

Although clearly not muscles, ligaments and tendons are soft tissues. Ligaments stabilise joints by joining bone to bone. With increased ligament strength, joints are less likely to dislocate, as the ligaments will be strong enough to hold the bones forming the joint in place. This means the performer can carry on training without fear of this injury.

Figure 12.2 Adaptations allow the rugby players to meet the demands of their sport, providing the strength, speed and power they need to be effective

Tendons attach muscle to bone; an increase in their strength again reduces the chance of injury and therefore the performer is less likely to suffer with overuse injuries or a ruptured tendon. This means they will be able to maintain training and manage heavier training loads with a reduced risk of injury.

The increase in the stores of the energy sources used in anaerobic respiration in the muscle also means that the muscles can produce greater amounts of energy very quickly so they can maintain fast, powerful movements for longer. The increased tolerance to lactic acid means that more lactate can build in the muscle and the blood, before having a negative effect on their performance. Again this means a performer would be able to work at high intensity for slightly longer.

Finally, through hypertrophy of fast twitch muscle fibres, the performer's muscular contractions can generate even more strength, assisting their performance. For example, with greater strength the rugby player is more able to break free from a tackle.

Skeletal system

Bones are living tissue. They reshape and rebuild themselves many times as you grow. Age, exercise and your diet will affect bone development.

As a result of taking part in weight-bearing or resistance exercise, such as walking, running, weight training, or games such as tennis or aerobics on a regular basis, your body will start to adapt to its increased workload. These adaptations are what you should refer to if asked about the effects of regular training on the skeletal system:

- Increased bone density.
- Increased strength of bones.
- Reduced risk of osteoporosis.

Osteoporosis is a disease of the bone that leads to an increased risk of fracture.

Although normally associated with older people, it can affect those in their twenties and can have a very negative impact on an individual's quality of life. Imagine breaking a bone every time you fell over, or cracking a rib because you coughed too hard when you had a cold. By increasing bone density, you increase the strength of the bone reducing the risk of fracturing the bone when participating in physical activity, whether it is as a result of the force you put on the bone in training, such as a weight lifter or other 'power' athlete, or withstanding the force exerted on you by others, for example, the rugby player in Figure 12.2.

Long-term training effects and benefits of exercise on the cardio-respiratory system

In the same way that the musculo-skeletal system will adapt to training, so will the cardio-respiratory system. If you continue to exercise aerobically on a regular basis, following the principles of training, your cardiovascular and respiratory systems will start to adapt to the increased workload.

> **Check your understanding**
>
> 3. What is the difference between aerobic and anaerobic exercise?

Cardiovascular system

These are the adaptations you will need to be familiar with:

- increased strength of heart muscle
- increased size of heart
- increased resting stroke volume
- drop in resting heart rate
- increased maximum cardiac output
- increased capillarisation
- increase in number of red blood cells
- quicker recovery rate after exercise to return to resting heart rate.

As the heart undergoes cardiac hypertrophy, muscle fibres increase in strength. This means that the muscular walls of the heart, in particular the left ventricle, can contract with more force. What impact will this have on the blood leaving the heart?

The increase in heart size allows the ventricles to stretch more, in turn this means they can hold more blood. Will this impact on heart rate or stroke volume?

As a result of an increase in the size and strength of the heart, resting stroke volume will increase. This is because more blood is available to be squeezed out of the heart (due to increased size) and the potential to squeeze harder (due to increased strength) so that more blood is ejected from the heart each time the heart beats.

Note how the adaptation is to resting stroke volume; this differentiation is made because a short-term effect of exercise could be an increase in stroke volume, (see Chapter 6). For example, stroke volume increases as we exercise to increase blood flow. However, reference to increased resting stroke volume tells us this is a long-term effect due to the heart's adaptations that are still in place even when we are not exercising.

The increase in resting stroke volume means our heart does not need to beat as fast to provide the required cardiac output (remember the equation: cardiac output = stroke volume x heart rate) therefore, another long-term training effect is a drop in resting heart rate. This means our maximum cardiac output will also increase. Can you work out why?

Not only are there adaptations to the heart but also to the rest of the cardiovascular system. The number of capillaries available for blood to flow through increases. This makes it easier for greater quantities of blood to reach the muscles and there is also an increase in the number of red blood cells circulating in the blood. Both of these adaptations are important in the transport of oxygen to the muscles and the removal of carbon dioxide. Increasing the speed that oxygen can be delivered, means the performer can work aerobically for longer. It also means they can recover quicker after exercise as oxygen can continue to flow quickly to the muscles.

Actions

Table 12.1 shows heart rate, stroke volume and cardiac output values for a 20-year-old man who took part in an 8-week aerobic training programme to increase his fitness.

Using Table 12.1, calculate the man's maximum cardiac output, to see the training effects, assuming the man is working at the upper limit of his aerobic target zone. (See Karvonen's formula on p. 88)

	Unfit prior to starting training programme	Training effects	After completion of 8-week aerobic training programme
Resting heart rate	80 bpm	Drop in resting heart rate	70 bpm
Resting stroke volume	62 ml/beat	Increase in stroke volume	71 ml/beat
Resting cardiac output	4.9 litres/min	No change to resting cardiac output	4.9 litres/min
Maximum cardiac output	9.9 litres/min	Increase in maximum cardiac output	?

Table 12.1 Training effects on maximum cardiac output

Changes to the body as a result of regular exercise can also bring about long-term health benefits. The long-term health benefits of exercise on the cardiovascular system are:

- drop in resting blood pressure (due to more elastic muscular wall of blood vessels)
- reduction in cholesterol levels
- reduction in likelihood of coronary heart failure
- reduction in likelihood of a stroke
- reduced risk of Type 2 diabetes.

Respiratory system

Long-term training effects on the respiratory system are:

- increased strength of diaphragm
- increased strength of the external intercostal muscles
- increased tidal volume
- increased vital capacity
- increased number of alveoli.

The benefit of these adaptations to the performer is that they become more efficient at taking air containing oxygen into the body and, because

> **Check your understanding**
>
> 4. State two long-term benefits of training due to adaptations to the cardiovascular system.
>
> 5. State what happens at the alveoli.

of the increased number of alveoli, they can exchange more oxygen at the lungs that can then be transported to the working muscles. As the blood takes the oxygen from the alveoli it can release the additional carbon dioxide that has been generated back to the lungs to be breathed out.

We can see that there are a lot of potential benefits from regular training both in terms of improving our performance through increased fitness but also in relation to our health. However, none of these adaptations or benefits will occur without the proper amount of rest and recovery after and between training sessions.

Actions

Copy the boxes in Figure 12.3 to explain a long-term training effect and benefit of exercise on the system indicated in the boxes and how this supports the performer when exercising.

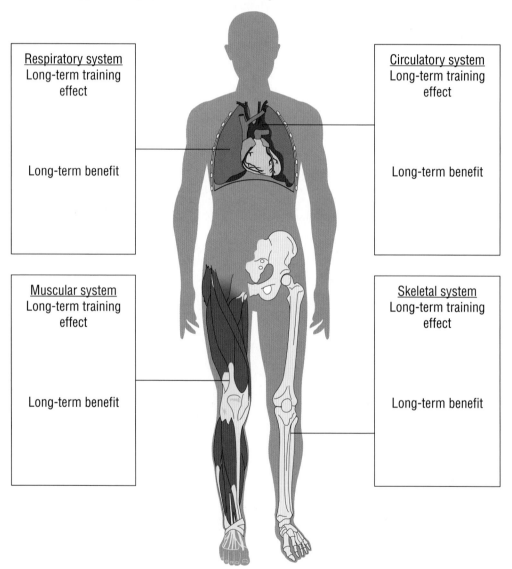

Figure 12.3 Long-term training effects and benefits of exercise on the body systems

PRACTICE QUESTIONS

1. Explain why an increase in the number of mitochondria could be beneficial to performance.

2. Identify one aerobic training adaptation to the muscular system.
   A increased strength of tendons
   B increased strength of ligaments
   C increased myoglobin content
   D increased muscle fatigue

3. Explain why osteoporosis is less likely in an individual that trains regularly.

4. Copy and complete Table 12.2 to state the long-term training effects on the cardio-respiratory system.

	Effect of long-term training
Resting heart rate	
Resting breathing rate	
Resting cardiac output	

Table 12.2

5. Explain the advantage of one long-term training effect on the respiratory system to a performer.

Summary

- Regular training causes the body systems to adapt to the exercise being carried out.
- The body systems that adapt to regular exercise are the:
  - skeletal system
  - muscular system
  - cardiovascular system
  - respiratory system.
- The adaptations to the body systems can also bring health benefits.

Useful websites

Adaptations to long term exercise – cardiovascular system
http://hubpages.com/health/Adaptations-to-long-term-exercise-Cardiovascular-System

Long-term effect of exercise – respiratory system
http://wccphysiologyunit.weebly.com/long-term-effects-of-exercise-respiratory-system.html

Long-term effect of exercise – muscular system
http://wccphysiologyunit.weebly.com/long-term-effects-of-exercise-muscular-system.html

Long-term effect of exercise – skeletal system
http://wccphysiologyunit.weebly.com/long-term-effects-of-exercise-skeleton.html

Study hints

Make sure you take all of the required information about the question from the introductory sentence. For example, question 2 is asking you to focus on aerobic training adaptations, so if an anaerobic adaptation is listed you can discount that option.

Chapter 13 Physical training – optimising training and preventing injury

Learning goals

By the end of this chapter you should be able to:

- identify common sports injuries
- describe the elements of RICE in the treatment of soft tissue injury
- explain injury prevention measures relating to a range of physical activities and sports including:
  - correct application of the principles of training to avoid overuse injuries
  - adherence to rules of an activity
  - use of appropriate protective clothing
  - use of appropriate protective equipment
  - checking of facilities and equipment before use
- explain the purpose and importance of a warm up and cool down
- describe the phases of a warm up and explain their importance
- give examples of activities included in warm ups and cool downs.

Key words

Sports injury – injuries that arise from taking part in sport or physical activity

Concussion – temporary brain injury due to a violent blow to the head or a fall

Fractures – a break or crack in a bone

Common sports injuries

The term sports injury refers to the kinds of injuries that commonly occur during sport or exercise. As we know, physical activity can be very beneficial to health as it reduces the risk of heart disease, stroke and obesity and helps to beat depression.

However, exercise can also cause injuries, particularly if you do not prepare properly, use the proper safety equipment or follow the rules of the activity. Look at Figure 13.1 to see some of the potential injuries that can be sustained through taking part in sport.

Concussion

Occasionally, sport performers will receive head injuries, for example, if two football players, jumping to head the ball, clash heads instead.

Knocking heads hard enough can cause the brain to bounce against the rigid bone of the cranium, which can cause concussion.

Fractures

Fractures occur as a result of direct or indirect force and tend to be associated with contact sports. For example, fractures of bones in the lower leg and foot can happen in football because of direct force, for example, being kicked. An example of an indirect force causing a fracture is when a player falls and puts their arms out to break their fall. The point of impact is at the wrist/hand, but the force travels along the arm to the shoulder and onto the clavicle that can then fracture.

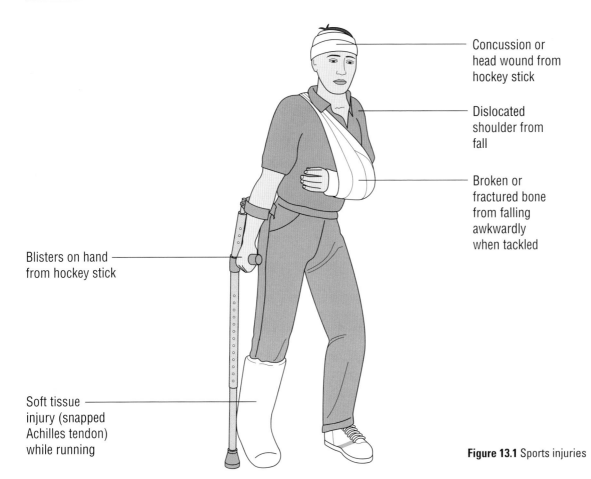

Concussion or head wound from hockey stick

Dislocated shoulder from fall

Broken or fractured bone from falling awkwardly when tackled

Blisters on hand from hockey stick

Soft tissue injury (snapped Achilles tendon) while running

Figure 13.1 Sports injuries

Figure 13.2 Concussion can occur if players clash heads

Dislocations

These occur at joints, where the bone is moved out of its normal position. Dislocations as a result of sports injuries tend to happen at the shoulder, thumb and finger but can, as we see in Figure 13.3, also occur at the ankle.

Key word

Dislocation – an injury at a joint where the bones are forced out of their normal position

Figure 13.3 Dislocations can occur as the result of a heavy force. Note the angle of this unfortunate player's ankle!

They occur as a result of a heavy force acting on the joint, for example, diving to score a try in rugby and falling on the shoulder.

Soft tissue injuries

Bone is made of a hard material, therefore anything that is not bone is called soft tissue. This refers to muscles, ligaments and tendons.

Soft tissue injuries are common in sport. Soft tissue injuries include:

- **Strains** – in athletics it is not unusual to see an athlete suddenly pull out of a race holding their hamstrings because of a strained (torn or pulled) muscle. This usually happens when a muscle is stretched beyond its limits and normally occurs where the tendon joins the muscle. See the sprinter in Figure 13.4.

Key word

Soft tissue – any part of the body that is not made up of bone

Figure 13.4 A sprinter's race is finished when they suffer a hamstring strain

- **Sprains** – affect ligaments rather than tendons; they occur at or near a joint and are caused by wrenching or twisting of a joint. A twisted ankle is an example of a sprain. It is often difficult to remember which type of injury is a sprain and which type a strain. You might find it useful to use the 't' in strain to remember that it matches the 't' in torn or tendon, therefore affecting muscles.

- **Torn cartilage** – is another common injury, particularly at the knee. The cartilage normally fits on the ends of the bones of the knee joint, but if the cartilage is damaged or begins to deteriorate with age, it can tear. The torn piece of cartilage moves in the joint and can become caught or wedged between the bones. If this happens, the knee becomes painful, difficult to move and swollen.

- **Tennis elbow** – this is an injury to the muscles of the forearm that allow you to extend your wrist and turn your palm upward and the tendon that attaches the muscle to the elbow joint. It is called tennis elbow because the injury is common in tennis – the action of extending your wrist and turning your palm upward is carried out when you play a backhand stroke. Poor technique or the wrong size of grip on a racket can cause tennis elbow because of the unnecessary force acting on the tissues.

- **Golfer's elbow** – this affects the muscles and tendons responsible for flexing the wrist and is an injury caused by overuse. The injury is referred to as golfer's elbow because it is associated with that sport. During a game, golfers need to bend the wrist repeatedly when striking the ball; this can result in golfer's elbow if players play too much. You can develop tennis elbow or golfer's elbow even if you do not play those sports.

- **Cuts and abrasions** – players who receive cuts that begin to bleed must stop playing immediately to have the cut dressed (covered). Cuts and abrasions or grazes are common in sport. Cuts can occur from contact

Figure 13.5 A cyclist in the Tour de France falls on the tarmac road and suffers cuts and abrasions

with opponents (for example, the studs on their boots), or just another body part (for example, a clash of heads). Grazes normally occur if players fall over on harsh surfaces (such as tarmac netball courts, all-weather hockey pitches or frozen fields). A graze takes off the top layers of the skin.

Soft tissue injuries can be treated using the RICE procedure:

- R – Rest : take a break from the activity. A doctor, nurse or physiotherapist will be able to suggest how long you should rest based on the severity of the injury.
- I – Ice: apply ice to the injured part (although not directly onto the skin).
- C – Compression: a bandage is wrapped around the injured part to reduce further swelling and to give support.
- E – Elevation: lift the injured part. This reduces blood flow to the injury, reducing the amount of bruising.

You would obviously be very unlucky to suffer all of these injuries, but even so you should try to minimise the risk of receiving any injuries. We have already discussed the need to carry out a physical readiness questionnaire, PARQ (see Chapter 10), before starting on a programme of physical activity, to reduce the risk of triggering health issues as a result of a known medical condition. Other ways to reduce the risk of injury and therefore contribute to your general well-being are identified below.

Risks associated with physical activity and sport and how to reduce these risks

Correct application of the principles of training to avoid overuse injuries

It is essential that performers leave enough time for rest and recovery between physical activity or sport sessions to ensure the body is fully recovered before working again, otherwise the body is more likely to become injured. Overuse injuries occur over time due to repetitive use (without adequate rest), for example, tennis elbow and shin splints.

Rules

Rules are in place so that we can all enjoy playing sport. They make the sport fair and encourage good sporting behaviour. Rules also help to protect us from injury and maintain our safety.

Actions

Identify three rules from one of your practical activities and explain how they can help protect you from injury during the game.

Check your understanding

1. How might the rules identified in Table 13.1 protect the players? Copy and complete the table.

Rule	Reduced risk of injury
No lifting stick above head height	
Checking players' studs in their boots before they go on the pitch	
Must wear shin guards in football	

Table 13.1 Safety rules

Rules are not the only way of protecting yourself and others from injury.
You need to use the correct:

- protective clothing
- equipment
- facilities.

Protective clothing

This is vital in some sports. For example, although the idea in hockey
is to stop the ball with your stick, it will hit your shin from time to time.
Depending on how hard the ball has been hit, this can be very painful
unless you are wearing shin guards. Similarly, players wear mouth guards
so that they do not lose their teeth if they are hit with a hockey stick
or ball.

Actions

Name the items of protective clothing in Figure 13.6, the sporting activity they would be associated with and explain
how they help reduce risk of injury.

Figure 13.6 Protective clothing

Actions

Look at the pictures in Figure 13.7. List the items of protective clothing, what they are being used to protect and the injury which they are designed to prevent.

Figure 13.7 What does the item of protective clothing protect and what risk is reduced?

Equipment

You should always check the equipment you are going to use. Ask yourself, is it safe for use? If the answer is no, do not use it. For example:

- Playing squash or badminton with an inappropriate grip on the handle could lead to the racket flying out of your hand. This might not result in an injury to you, but could mean that a partner or opponent is hit with the racket.
- In basketball, if the hoop is damaged the court should not be used until it is fixed, otherwise it could fall and injure those underneath it.
- In netball, the goal posts should be checked to make sure the bolts securing the hoops are tight.
- The equipment you use may also need some protective clothing! For example, rugby posts have padding around them so that if players run into the posts in the heat of the game, the risk of injury is reduced.

Facilities

The correct facilities also need to be used for the sport that you are playing. Sports halls can be used for a variety of activities, such as badminton, five-a-side football, netball, volleyball and table tennis, but if there is water on the floor making it slippery, the risk of injury is increased. Activities such as sprinting, however, should not be carried out in a sports hall unless the sprint stops well short of the end wall, or appropriate padding is placed at the end of the wall. Failure to do this would increase the risk of injury as sprinters could hit the end wall at pace, which could result in a broken bone. If rugby were played indoors, the rules about tackling would need to change, otherwise the risk of injury when players hit the hard floor would be too great.

Other points to consider about facilities include:

- trampolining should only be carried out if the height of the facility allows it
- rugby matches should be cancelled if the pitch is frozen
- outdoor netball matches should be cancelled if the court is too icy
- long jump pits should always be checked for 'unwanted objects' before use.

Actions

Identify two checks you would carry out on the facilities before taking part in one of your practical activities for assessment (see Chapter 24) and explain why.

Actions

Work with a partner and think about what issues you should consider regarding facilities for the following activities:
- basketball
- swimming
- discus
- boxing.

Figure 13.8 Padding around chair lifts on ski runs

Check your understanding

2. What items of safety equipment are used, or what checks to the equipment should be carried out to reduce risk of injury during a trampolining session?

Figure 13.9 Long jump pits should be checked before use

Actions

Look at the pictures in Figure 13.10. Identify some of the risks and the possible precautions against those risks for each sporting activity. Copy Table 13.2, enter your answers and discuss them with others in your group.

Figure 13.10 What are the risks?

Sport	Risk – what could happen when participating in this activity?	How could you reduce the risk? What is the risk reduction measure?
Netball		
White-water rafting		
1500 m		
Rugby		
Gymnastics		
Rock climbing		

Table 13.2 Risks and risk reduction measures

Warm-ups and cool-downs

Any exercise session, whatever the sporting activity, should involve a warm-up before the main activity and a cool-down after it. There are good reasons for this.

The warm-up is used to prepare the body for the activity you are about to take part in. It should help you physically and mentally. The cool-down helps return the body to a resting state.

Warm-up

A proper warm-up has many benefits:

- Muscles are ready for exercise as they will be able to contract and relax more quickly.

- Oxygen will be more easily available to the muscles because of the increased heart rate.

- Muscle fibres will become more elastic and therefore less likely to tear.

- The performer becomes more focused on the task they are about to undertake – it forms part of their psychological preparation.

Warm-ups will also help reduce the risk of injury: you can ensure that muscles and tendons are ready for action by gently increasing the amount of work they do, rather than just going from static to very active in one step. Therefore, by using a properly planned warm-up, the performer is less likely to receive a sprain or strain.

A warm-up has three phases:

- Pulse raising/increasing body temperature – this is achieved by completing some form of light, continuous activity, such as jogging.

- Stretching, achieved through stretching! You should start from the top and work down, stretching the muscles that will be worked in the main

Check your understanding

3. Which of the activities pictured in Figure 13.10 presents the greatest risk? Justify your answer.

Figure 13.11 The three phases of a warm up

Check your understanding

4. What phase of the warm-up is the basketball player in Figure 13.12 completing?

Figure 13.12 Which phase of the warm-up?

5. Why is it important to maintain blood flow as part of the cool-down at the end of an intense exercise session rather than just stop exercising?

session. The value of stretching is to increase the range of movement possible at the joint.

● Event-specific drills to prepare your body for the activity you are about to do, for example, dribbling or passing skills, dodging or tackling skills or serving or bowling skills.

Actions

Research different warm-up activities and ask your teacher if you can take the warm-up, or at least part of it, in your next practical session.

An internet site that might provide some ideas is:
Warm-up ideas
http://www.teachingideas.co.uk:80/pe/contents.htm

Actions

Identify three drills you could do in the final part of a warm up for one of your own practical activities.

Cool-down

Cool-downs do not reduce the risk of injury during performance, but they do reduce the risk of muscle stiffness after performance and speed up the removal of lactic acid. They also reduce the risk of fainting after activity by keeping the blood circulating back to the heart and gradually reducing the heart rate – the heart rate should be brought down to within 15 bpm of the resting heart rate.

A cool-down has two phases:

● A reduction in body temperature, slow jogging/walking to bring down the level of activity gradually and help removal of carbon dioxide and lactic acid.

● More stretching to help reduce temperature slowly, to assist in the removal of waste products and to stretch the muscles after they have been working to increase the range of movement possible at the joint.

Study hints

If a question asks for a common injury, make sure you go with the most obvious answer, as this will be the required answer.

PRACTICE QUESTIONS

1. Name a common sports injury associated with sprinting.

2. What are soft tissue injuries?

3. Describe the treatment for a soft tissue injury.

4. Explain two risk reduction measures for your sport.

5. Which phase of a warm-up is not needed in a cool-down and why?

Summary

- Participation in physical activity and sport can cause common sports injuries.
- Risk reduction measures to reduce injury in physical activity and sport include:
  - correct application of the principles of training to avoid overuse injuries
  - adherence to rules of an activity
  - use of appropriate protective clothing
  - use of appropriate protective equipment
  - checking of facilities and equipment before use.
- RICE is used in the treatment of soft tissue injury.
- A warm-up is used to prepare physically and psychologically for performance.
- A warm-up has three clear phases.
- A cool-down helps to gradually reduce heart rate.

Useful websites

Alphabetical list of common sports injuries and pain
http://sportsmedicine.about.com/cs/injuries/a/alphainjurylist.htm

Sports injuries
https://www.betterhealth.vic.gov.au/health/healthyliving/sports-injuries

Preventing musculoskeletal sports injuries in youth: A guide for parents
www.niams.nih.gov/Health_info/Sports_Injuries/child_sports_injuries.asp#most

Chapter 14 Physical training – performance-enhancing drugs

Learning goals

By the end of this chapter you should be able to:

- name different types of performance-enhancing drugs
- explain the positive effects of these classes of drugs on sporting performance
- explain the negative effects of these classes of drugs on sporting performance.

Key words

Performance-enhancing drugs (PEDs) – supplements taken by an athlete so that they can perform better due to additional or enhanced training adaptations brought about by the drug

WADA – World Anti-Doping Agency

The classes of performance-enhancing drugs (PEDs)

Elite performers dedicate their lives to becoming as good as they can possibly be and hopefully the best in their chosen activity. They are under huge amounts of pressure to find ways to increase their performance and for some the pressure is so great that they turn to performance-enhancing drugs – drugs that will help them perform to an even higher standard in their sport.

The problem with this is that the use of PEDs is banned and considered to be cheating, so anyone found taking drugs would be disqualified. The two main reasons they are banned are:

- they artificially improve your performance, so if you take them you are cheating
- taking the drugs may improve performance, but they also present dangerous side effects, which the athletes should be protected from.

The World Anti-Doping Agency (WADA – see useful websites box) is responsible for testing athletes before, during and after major sporting events to check that the performers are 'clean'. Despite ideals, such as the Olympic Oath, testing of athletes is still required because performers are still tempted to take PEDs. BBC Sport reported that of the 283,304 drugs tests carried out worldwide in 2013, 3,800 contained banned substances. WADA reported that more than 10% of elite athletes could be using PEDs.

Performance-enhancing drugs and methods are grouped into classes or types of drugs; those with similar effects on performance are grouped together. There are nearly 200 different banned classes of drugs or methods on WADA's prohibited list. The list contains classes of drugs and some examples.

Table 14.1 shows:

- six classes of PEDs
- two specific examples of the drug class peptide hormones
- one performance-enhancing method.

PED CLASS	EXAMPLES OF PED CLASS REQUIRED	PERFORMANCE-ENHANCING METHOD
Anabolic steroids	x	x
Beta blockers	x	x
Diuretics	x	x
Narcotic analgesics	x	x
Peptide hormones	Erythropoietin (EPO) Growth hormones (GH)	x
Stimulants	x	x
Banned method	x	Blood doping

Table 14.1 Banned PEDs and methods

You will need to know about all of these for your assessment. The X's in the Table show you do not need to know specific examples for these classes of drugs, or that the class of drug is not a doping method.

Actions

Carry out some research on a recent major sporting event, such as the Olympics, Fifa World Cup or World Athletics championship, to find out whether any athletes were accused of taking PEDs. Copy the table and record the following information to complete the first three columns of Table 14.2: the name of the performer, the sporting activity and the class of drug taken.

1. Performer	2. Sporting activity	3. Class of drug accused of taking	4. How would it improve performance?	5. Possible harmful side effects of this type of drug

Table 14.2

Positive effects of PEDs

Anabolic steroids

Performers take this drug so they can train harder and for longer. With increased intensity of training they will make better gains in strength and power. They will also be advantaged as muscle recovery after training will be quicker and the body will lose fat.

Beta blockers

These have a calm and relaxing effect on the individual; they slow the body systems down, for example, reduce heart rate. Most importantly,

Check your understanding

1. Identify a banned performance-enhancing method.

Key words

Anabolic steroid – synthetic hormone resembling testosterone, used to promote muscle growth

Beta blockers – used to control heart rhythm

Key words

Diuretics – a drug that reduces the amount of water in the body

Narcotic analgesics – drugs used to suppress pain

Peptide hormones – protein hormones naturally occurring in the body

Stimulants – something that raises the nervous activity of the body

Actions

Look at the positive effects of each class of drug – who would benefit from taking these drugs? Match one activity to each class of drug and explain how this would aid performance in that activity. Check your answers with a partner.

Check your understanding

2. State one advantage of stimulants.

3. In which activity would performers benefit most from EPO?

4. Why would a performer take narcotic analgesics?

they can reduce muscle tremor, therefore they are very important in precision sports.

Diuretics

These are useful if the performer needs quick weight loss, if their weight is critical to allow them to compete, for example, boxers. If they are a couple of pounds overweight, they can take diuretics so they can 'make weight' for their specific weight category. Also, as urine is passed sooner, if other drugs have been taken, for example, anabolic steroids, the 'evidence' (the trace amounts in the urine used in testing) is removed from the body sooner. This means that the performer may be able to remove traces of drug taking from their body sooner, before they can be tested and caught for cheating. It is for this reason that many different types of athletes may take this drug to mask the fact they have taken another PED.

Narcotic analgesics

These are taken by performers to reduce any pain they may feel from an injury. Therefore, this drug helps the performer 'hide' the injury from managers or coaches so they can play and also from themselves. As the athlete feels no pain from the injury they feel well enough to continue to train hard.

Peptide hormones

These alter the natural state of the body by changing the bodies hormone balance. For example, erythropoietin (EPO) increases the red blood cell count and therefore increases the oxygen-carrying capacity of the blood. This would be advantageous in endurance events where performers need the extra oxygen to continue to work hard. Growth hormone (hGH) is another example of a peptide hormone; it increases muscle size and strength and decreases body fat and therefore has similar effects to anabolic steroids.

Stimulants

These increase the performer's physical or mental alertness. They become more aware and their senses are heightened. Stimulants can also increase the performer's confidence in their ability to do well, giving them greater competitiveness so they try even harder to win.

Actions

Look at the named performers and their activities in Table 14.3 – all of these performers tested positive in a drugs test. What physical advantage were they hoping to gain? Copy and complete the table.

Athlete	Physical activity	Drug taken	Possible physical advantage?
Tyson Gay	Sprinter	Anabolic steroids	
Abderrahim Goumri	Marathon runner	Blood doping	
Mariem Alaoui Selsouli	1500 m runner	Diuretic	
Nadzeya Ostapchuk	Shot-put	Anabolic steroids	
Kissya Cataldo	Single sculls	EPO	

Table 14.3 Athletes who have tested positive in drugs tests

Negative effects of PEDs

One of the main reasons for banning PEDs is due to the health risks they can present if taken long-term. Some of these negative side effects are stated in Table 14.4.

PERFORMANCE-ENHANCING DRUG	SPECIFIC EXAMPLES OF NEGATIVE EFFECTS OF PERFORMANCE-ENHANCING DRUGS
Anabolic steroids	Liver dysfunction Kidney tumours High blood pressure Premature heart disease Aggression Depression Acne Low sperm count Abnormal menstrual cycles
Beta blockers	Sleep disturbance and therefore tiredness Low blood pressure Drop in heart rate
Diuretics	Dehydration Nausea Headaches Drop in blood pressure Heart/kidney/liver failure
Narcotic analgesics	Nausea and vomiting Loss of concentration Loss of balance/co-ordination May lead to permanent injury Addiction
Peptide hormones Erythropoietin (EPO)	Increased viscosity of blood therefore increased risk of heart failure/stroke Deep vein thrombosis Pulmonary embolism Death
Growth hormones (hGH)	Arthritis Brain swelling Heart failure Osteoporosis Impotence Abnormal menstrual cycles
Stimulants	Aggression Anxiety Insomnia Irregular and increased heart rate Increased blood pressure Inhibited judgement Hand tremor Addiction

(cont.)

(cont.)

PERFORMANCE-ENHANCING DRUG	SPECIFIC EXAMPLES OF NEGATIVE EFFECTS OF PERFORMANCE-ENHANCING DRUGS
Blood doping	Blood poisoning
	Cardiac output decrease
	Contraction of infectious diseases, e.g. HIV
	Heart failure
	High blood pressure
	Kidney damage
	Thrombosis

Table 14.4 Negative effects of performance-enhancing drugs

Check your understanding

5. State **two** reasons why performers should not take PEDs.

Actions

Go back to Table 14.2 and complete:

- column 4 by giving an example of a way in which their performance may have benefited by taking this drug
- column 5 by giving a harmful side effect that they may experience as a result.

PRACTICE QUESTIONS

1. Copy the table below. Draw two lines to link each class of drugs to a relevant side effect.

Drug	Side Effect
Beta blockers	Liver/kidney failure
	Deep vein thrombosis
	Low blood pressure
Diuretics	High blood pressure
	Increased risk of heart failure

2. Explain why, despite the risks, some sports performers still take anabolic steroids.

3. Explain one risk associated with diuretics.

4. Which **one** of the following performers is most likely to take a beta blocker?

   A 100 m sprinter

   B A footballer

   C An archer

   D A downhill skier

5. Explain **one** activity where performers may engage in blood doping.

Study hints

Think about the effects of blood doping. Who would benefit most from these effects in their sport?

Summary

- The classes of performance-enhancing drugs include:
  - anabolic steroids
  - beta blockers
  - diuretics
  - narcotic analgesics
  - peptide hormones
  - stimulants.
- EPO and hGH are examples of peptide hormones.
- Blood doping is a banned method of enhancing performance.
- Performance-enhancing drugs are taken for the advantage they give the performer.
- Each class of performance-enhancing drug carries a different set of health risks for the performer.

Useful websites

The story of anti-doping
www.ukad.org.uk/new-to-anti-doping/story-of-anti-doping/

World Anti-Doping Agency
www.wada-ama.org

Effects of PEDs
www.usada.org/substances/effects-of-performance-enhancing-drugs/

Chapter 15 Health, fitness and well-being

Improving physical, emotional and social health, fitness and well-being through physical activity

Individuals join clubs and take part in physical activity for the benefits it can bring. Probably the best way to understand this is to think about your own and other people's reasons for taking part.

The benefits of physical activity are normally grouped as follows:

- emotional – to do with the mind, our psychological health
- physical – to do with the body, our physical health
- social – to do with the way we interact with others, our social health.

Figure 15.1 What benefits do you think this group get from participating in physical activity?

Very often benefits can overlap from one category to another. For example, if you were overweight you might take part in physical activity to lose some weight. This has an obvious physical benefit (you lose excess weight), but could also have an emotional benefit (you feel better about yourself because you are not so worried about being overweight and you are becoming physically healthier).

In your exam you might be asked to list some benefits of physical activity and categorise them. It is also likely that you will be expected to explain how physical activity actually brings about any benefits you claim it has. For example, one benefit of physical activity is feeling good. This is an emotional benefit. One explanation for this is that when exercising aerobically researchers believe there is an increase in the levels of serotonin (a chemical) in the brain – this chemical provides a feel-good factor altering our mood to a more positive one. Because this feeling of well-being is associated with aerobic exercise it is sometimes referred to as 'runner's high' or 'jogger's high'. Have you experienced this 'feel-good' factor after aerobic activity?

Actions

Copy Table 15.1 and use it to list the reasons you have for taking part in physical activity (try to think of at least four reasons).

Reason/benefit from participation in physical activity or sport

Table 15.1 My reasons for taking part in physical activity or sport

Actions

Compare your list with another person's list from your group and add any relevant different answers from their list to your list.

Actions

Copy Table 15.2. Compare your combined list with the list in Table 15.2. This list was also created by a group of PE students. Have they identified any different benefits? Working on your own or with a partner, look at Table 15.2 and categorise each of the benefits as a physical, social or emotional benefit of physical activity. How many of the benefits could have appeared under more than one category?

Reason/benefit from participation in physical activity or sport	Category of benefit
Lose excess weight	Physical
Relieves my stress/helps me to relax	
I need a physical challenge	
I am good at it	
Gives me better muscle definition	
Improves my health	
Gives me something to do	
Makes me feel good	
I develop an aesthetic appreciation of the sport	
I like to compete	
Meet my friends	
Stops me getting into trouble/bored	
Good way of meeting boys/girls	
Helps me to learn how to co-operate with others	
Improves my fitness	
Increases my confidence/self-esteem	

Table 15.2 Reasons for taking part in physical activity or sport

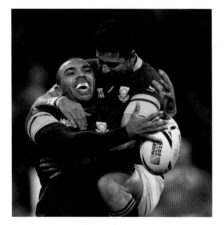

Figure 15.2 Benefits from physical activity and sport

Actions

Compare your answers from Table 15.2 with those given in Table 15.3.

Reason/benefit from participation in physical activity or sport	Category of benefit
Lose excess weight	Physical
Relieves my stress/helps me to relax	Emotional
I need a physical challenge	Physical or emotional
I am good at it	Emotional
Gives me better muscle definition	Physical
Improves my health	Physical
Gives me something to do	Emotional
Makes me feel good	Emotional
I develop an aesthetic appreciation of the sport	Emotional
I like to compete	Emotional
Meet my friends	Social
Stops me getting into trouble	Social
Good way of meeting boys/girls	Social
Helps me to learn how to co-operate with others	Social
Improves my fitness	Physical
Increases my confidence/self-esteem	Emotional

Table 15.3 Categorising the reasons for taking part in physical activity or sport

Actions

Look at Table 15.3 and try to explain how physical activity could bring about each of the stated benefits.

Compare your explanations with those given in Table 15.4.

Reason/benefit from participation in physical activity or sport	Category of benefit	How benefit is achieved
Lose excess weight	Physical	Doing more exercise than normal, so burning off more calories to reduce weight
Relieves my stress/helps me to relax	Emotional	By taking my mind off the things that are worrying me
I need a physical challenge	Physical or emotional	Physical – increase in fitness as a result of the additional physical work. Emotional – sense of achievement gained from doing something physical. Very important for those who do little physically during their normal day, e.g. people who work in offices. One reason why events such as the London Marathon are so popular is because people enjoy the physical challenge of training this type of event

(cont.)

I am good at it	Emotional	Can improve people's confidence/self-esteem if they are seen as 'good' at something, especially if they are not viewed in this way at other times
Gives me better muscle definition	Physical	Through continued use, muscles can develop strength and fat stores can be depleted (with an appropriate diet and training programme). Both of these factors would make the muscles easier to see (clearer muscle definition)
Improves my health	Physical	There are many possible physical health benefits to exercise, e.g. reduction in blood pressure and cholesterol, reduction in chances of weight-related illness
Gives me something to do/stops me being bored	Emotional	With something positive to do that you enjoy, you are unlikely to feel bored
Makes me feel good	Emotional	You feel good for a number of reasons: you are having fun, you enjoy the challenge, you are not bored and possibly because of the endorphins released or increased serotonin levels when involved in long, continuous exercise
I develop an aesthetic appreciation of the sport	Emotional	Most people enjoy watching a skilful performance and can appreciate the 'beauty' of that performance. This does not just refer to activities such as gymnastics or dance; it can be equally valid when watching skilful play in rugby or football too
I like to compete	Emotional	I feel good if I win; it allows me to focus on something else and use up some of my energy
Meet my friends	Social	My friends play the same sport as I do, so I see them at training or matches
Stops me getting into trouble	Social	By stopping me getting bored (emotional) and giving me something definite to do
Good way of meeting boys/girls	Social	Members of the opposite sex play sport and it is a good way of meeting people with similar interests
Helps me to learn how to co-operate with others	Social	Through working with team mates, coaches and other members of the club I learn how to co-operate with others
Improves my fitness	Physical	Regular training will result in the body adapting to the new level of work we are asking it to do. These changes could include increased strength, cardiovascular endurance and many more, and are discussed in more detail in Chapter 12
Increases my confidence/self-esteem	Emotional	Playing sport regularly may mean that you get better at it, you may increase your fitness and you may make some good friends. All of these things contribute to you feeling better about yourself

Table 15.4 Reasons why the benefits from physical activity and sport may be achieved

Social and emotional benefits can occur on a fairly immediate basis. This means that you can gain these benefits the first time you participate in a sport. For example, you have gone to a taster badminton session and make some new friends and have fun – it has only taken one session for you to feel these benefits. However, the physical benefits will take longer to take place; time will be needed for the body to adapt to new levels of exercise (see Chapter 12). If fitness and long-term health gains are what you are after you will need to design, develop, carry out, monitor and adapt a suitable personal exercise programme (PEP) as outlined in Chapters 11 and 24.

Actions

1. Interview people from other age groups and the opposite gender to you (these should be family members, friends, friends' families and peers at school other than your PE class) to see why they take part in physical activity.
2. Categorise their answers as emotional, physical or social and explain how these benefits are achieved.
3. Draw graphs to represent the data you have collected and present your findings to the rest of the group.

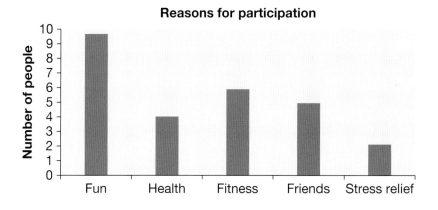

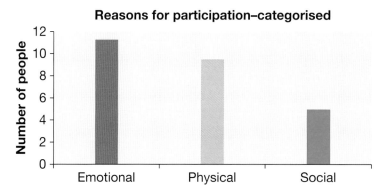

Figure 15.3 Ways to present data

1. State the three components of health.
2. Give two physical health benefits from participation in physical activity.
3. Which of these is a social benefit of participation in physical activity?

A – Increased self-esteem

B – Aesthetic appreciation

C – Physical challenge

D – Co-operation

Key words

Lifestyle choice – the choices we make about how we live and behave that impact on our health

Lifestyle choices

There are lots of things that we have to do on a day-to-day basis, like go to work or school, but we also have choices over some of the things we do. We can make decisions about:

- our diet
- whether we smoke
- how much alcohol we consume
- how active we are
- how long we spend working
- how long we spend resting
- how long we spend sleeping.

Actions

What choices have you already made today that could impact on your health? Work with a partner and go through your day; is there anything you could have done differently? Have all your choices been good ones as far as your health is concerned?

Actions

How good are your choices in relation to this list of lifestyle choices? Think back to the last couple of days and copy and complete Table 15.5. You may need to use the internet to work out the number of calories eaten.

The NHS has a useful calorie counter as part of its website: http://www.nhs.uk/Livewell/weight-loss-guide/Pages/calorie-counting.aspx

Lifestyle choice	My choices
Diet – number of calories	
Diet – healthy choices	
Number of cigarettes smoked	
Alcohol consumption	
Activity – how much and how hard	
Time at work	
Time at play	
Time sleeping	

Table 15.5 My lifestyle choices

Actions

Now compare your choices with Government recommendations. Are you making good choices? Can the same be said for your family? Have a look at Table 15.6 and indicate yes or no to each of the lifestyle choices. Do you need to make any significant changes to come in line with the government recommendations? If you do, be warned, research shows that it can take as long as three months before benefits from any changes can be seen, so you will need to be motivated if a change is needed.

Lifestyle Choice	Guidelines (Government, NHS, sleep foundation)	Yes/No
Diet – number of calories	Men – 2500 calorie intake daily	
	Women – 2000 calorie intake daily	
	Remember this will be affected by several factors, e.g. age, (teenagers often need more energy), how active you are, your size	
Diet – healthy choices	Eat a wide range of foods	
	Most of your calories should come from carbohydrates – pasta, potatoes, rice	
	Eat five portions of fruit and veg a day	
	Two portions of fish a week	
	Try to eat unsaturated fat rather than saturated, e.g. reduced fat spread rather than butter, non-fatty meat	
	Limit sugar on cereals and in drinks	
	Eat less than 6 g of salt a day	
Number of cigarettes smoked	Aim for 0, but smoking has a cumulative effect – someone who smokes two cigarettes is more at risk than someone who smokes one	
Alcohol consumption	No more than 14 units of alcohol per week	
Activity – how much and how hard (up to 18)	60 minutes of physical activity every day	
	3 days a week this should focus on developing bone strength, i.e. weight-bearing exercise	
Time at work	The government states that people should not normally work more than 48 hours a week	
Time sleeping	The recommendation from the sleep foundation is that you have 8–10 hours per night	
Time at play	If 10 hours is spent sleeping and 9.5 hours spent working that leaves you 4.5 hours 'free time' per day	

Table 15.6 Government recommendations

Actions

Research ways the government tries to help people to
- increase activity levels
- stop smoking
- eat more healthily
- reduce alcohol consumption.

Positive and negative impact of lifestyle choices

Diet

Regularly eating more calories than the body needs for the amount of physical work it is doing will lead to weight gain. Eventually, if left unchecked this will result in obesity and an increased risk of all the other health issues associated with obesity (see next section on sedentary lifestyles).

Figure 15.4 Use of exercise to reduce obesity

Some obese people, as shown in Figure 15.4, take part in low levels of physical exercise as part of a programme to help them change their lifestyle. By increasing energy output through exercise some weight will be lost, especially if this is coupled with a reduced calorie diet appropriate to the individual.

Obesity is not the only issue with poor lifestyle choices in relation to diet. Some people do not eat enough to support the day-to-day needs of their body. These individuals risk becoming anorexic. This is an eating disorder brought about through a distorted impression of self-image and low self-esteem. In other words, someone who clearly does not need to lose weight believes they are fat and so voluntarily 'starves' in an attempt to lose weight. The problem is because they have a distorted impression of how they really look they are starving the body of essential nutrients and seriously damaging their health. This condition (if left unchecked) will result in hospitalisation or death.

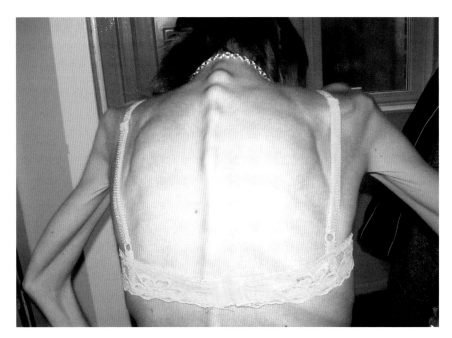

Figure 15.5 The anorexic body of a 17-year-old, weighing just under 5 stone

Table 15.7 shows the increasing cases of eating disorders that were diagnosed and admitted to English NHS hospitals between 2005 and 2014.

YEAR	HOSPITAL ADMISSIONS DUE TO EATING DISORDERS (PER 100,000)
2005–06	1,882
2006–07	1,924
2007–08	1,872
2008–09	1,868
2009–10	2,067
2010–11	No data available
2011–12	2,285
2012–13	2,380
1013–14	2,855

Table 15.7 Number of hospital admissions due to eating disorders in England

Source: www.b-eat.co.uk

The right diet can have a positive impact on our lives. Coupled with other positive lifestyle choices:

- we reduce the risk of many health-related diseases
- we have sufficient energy to carry out our daily routine
- we feel better emotionally due to feeling healthier.

Key words

Passive smoking – breathing in the harmful effects of someone else's smoke

Actions

1. Research smoking statistics on the British Medical Associations website (see Useful websites box).
2. Produce pie charts to show:
   - the percentage of adult smokers in the Home Nations (England, Scotland, Wales and Northern Ireland)
   - the estimated number of people that die each year from tobacco related illnesses in each Home Nation.
3. Analyse and comment on the data from the pie charts.

Smoking

The effects of smoking are well documented and various governments over the years have tried to reduce the appeal of smoking to encourage people to quit.

Some of the measures brought in include:

- banning the advertising of cigarettes on the television
- banning the use of cigarette based sponsorship for sports seen on the television
- a ban on smoking in public places (2007)
- a ban on smoking in private cars if young people over the age of 18 are also in the car (2015).

The reason governments get involved is because of the health risk associated with smoking. Even those passively smoking have an increased risk of asthma and meningitis, in addition to cancer.

If you smoke, you are two to three times more likely to have a heart attack than a non-smoker and much more likely to die from heart disease. Smokers are also more likely to have strokes, blood clots and angina.

Tobacco smoking can result in respiratory diseases like lung cancer, emphysema and chronic bronchitis, and leaves sufferers breathless and unable to do much activity.

As a smoker, your risk of developing diabetes in adult life is two to three times higher than that of a non-smoker.

Tobacco contains nicotine, which is addictive. This is why giving up smoking is so difficult, even though people know the risks of continuing.

Apart from the obvious health risks, smoking will decrease performance in practical activity due to the carbon monoxide contained in cigarette smoke. The haemoglobin in the red blood cells that is normally used to carry oxygen will carry carbon monoxide in preference, reducing the amount of oxygen available to release energy and the performer's ability to work aerobically. Heavy smokers may have as much as ten per cent of their haemoglobin bound by carbon monoxide. This obviously has more of an effect on performers in endurance events, but will affect the recovery of all performers.

Alcohol

Many people drink moderate amounts of alcohol to be sociable. The immediate effects of alcohol vary depending on the amount consumed and therefore the amount of alcohol in the blood. If low amounts of alcohol are consumed you can witness the following effects:

- relaxes the drinker
- reduces tension
- lowers inhibitions
- impairs concentration
- slows reflexes
- impairs reaction time
- reduces co-ordination
- causes loss of balance.

While the first two bullet points might release stress, the last five points will have a negative impact on performance. As a result, alcohol should not be drunk before sporting activity. Like nicotine, alcohol can become addictive.

Long-term effects of drinking too much alcohol include:

- increased weight (due to the calories in alcohol)
- cancer of the liver and/or bowel
- heart failure
- high blood pressure.

Activity level

Regular appropriate physical activity can help protect us from:

- obesity
- coronary heart disease
- strokes
- high blood pressure
- Type 2 diabetes
- colon cancer
- breast cancer
- osteoporosis
- depression
- insomnia.

But don't forget too much physical activity, without appropriate rest, can lead to negative effects, such as overtraining.

Sleep

An appropriate amount of sleep is essential to allow our brains time to recover from the day, to strengthen connections built in the brain as a result of a new experience or to remove unnecessary connections. A lack of sleep can lead to:

- increased risk of heart disease
- high blood pressure
- increased risk of stroke
- parts of the brain being temporarily inactive ('asleep'), even though we are awake
- being more likely to have a car accident due to falling asleep while driving.

Our bodies also benefit from sleep, as while they are sleeping body systems can recover physically from the day's work.

Due to modern technology our sleep patterns are changing. We can stay up longer because we have the means to provide light even though it is dark outside. We have electronic devices that, due to the bright light source, make it harder for us to sleep if we have looked at them just before going to bed, for example, an electronic book or mobile phone.

Figure 15.6 Using electronic devices can make it harder to get to sleep due to the bright light they emit

The consequences of a sedentary lifestyle

One of the problems of our modern society is that it is too easy not to exercise, in fact sometimes it is difficult to do so. This is in part because:

- most adults have access to a car or public transport therefore they do not need to walk to get to and from places
- most adults have sedentary jobs, for example, a job where they sit behind a desk all day
- most adults, due to fatigue, sit down when they get home from work, this is made more attractive as entertainment is available via the television.

Figure 15.7 The quality and accessibility of home entertainment encourages sedentary use of leisure time

Research into sedentary lifestyles now focuses on the effect of sitting for long periods of time. Researchers are concerned that even if you exercise regularly after work, if you are sitting for seven hours a day this is bad for your health. Researchers from Loughborough University and the University of Leicester collected data from almost 800,000 people across the world and looked at the link between time spent sitting down and increased health risks. This research found that there was a much greater risk of:

- diabetes
- cardiovascular disease
- increased risk of death due to cardiovascular disease
- increased risk of death from any health issue.

This research recommends that people stand for at least two hours a day. Sitting spells should be limited to 30 minutes. There should then be an active break, which could be standing for a minute.

Figure 15.8 Much of today's work opportunities involve sitting for most of the day

Figure 15.9 Research suggests that standing at a computer is better for our health than sitting for long periods of time

The consequences of a sedentary lifestyle are severe, with an increased risk of:

- becoming overweight – as we are not using all the calories we eat
- becoming overfat – as we continue to gain weight, which, if left unchecked, could lead to obesity
- high blood pressure – due to an increase in cholesterol associated with increased weight
- obesity – exercise helps regulate insulin levels, improving your use of insulin, therefore this will not happen if we do not exercise
- coronary heart disease – due to high blood pressure and cholesterol
- reduced life expectancy – due to coronary heart disease
- osteoporosis – as lack of exercise means bone density is not improved (weight bearing)
- loss of muscle tone – due to lack of use of muscles, previous training effects are lost if muscles are not used
- poor posture – due to loss of muscle tone
- negative impact on fitness components – as not exercising. Remember our bodies only improve if we train to cope with the additional demands; if there are no demands they do not need to adapt and improve.

PRACTICE QUESTIONS

1. Which of these is an emotional benefit of participation in physical activity?
   A Meet new friends
   B Increased self-esteem
   C Reduction in crime
   D Co-operation

Study hints

When deciding on a category of benefit, use the 'obvious' category; don't try to make this too complicated. If related to other people classify as social; mental health link to emotional and the rest is physical!

PRACTICE QUESTIONS

2. Analyse the data in Figure 15.3 to determine the most popular reason for participation.

3. Look at Table 15.7.

    (a) What happened to the hospital admissions for patients with eating disorders between 2006 and 2008?

    (b) Analyse whether the data for 2006 to 2008 is typical of the overall trend in those being hospitalised for eating disorders.

4. Activity level is a lifestyle choice. Discuss the impact of increasing your activity level above the daily recommended amount.

5. Explain one of the problems associated with a sedentary lifestyle.

Summary

- Physical activity can increase:
    - physical health
    - emotional health
    - social health.
- Lifestyle choices can have a positive impact on health, fitness and well-being.
- Poor lifestyle choices can have a negative impact on health, fitness and well-being.
- A sedentary lifestyle will have a negative impact on health, fitness and well-being.

Useful websites

Calorie checker
http://www.nhs.uk/Livewell/weight-loss-guide/Pages/calorie-counting.aspx

Beating eating disorders
www.b-eat.co.uk

BMA Smoking statistics
http://bma.org.uk/working-for-change/improving-and-protecting-health/tobacco/smoking-statistics

Get Britain Standing
http://www.getbritainstanding.org

Chapter 16 Energy, diet, nutrition and hydration for physical activity

Learning goals

By the end of this chapter you should be able to:

- state the requirements of a balanced diet
- explain the role and importance of macronutrients and micronutrients
- explain how sporting activity can affect nutritional requirements, including energy balance, carbohydrate loading, timing of protein intake and hydration levels
- state the factors affecting optimum weight
- explain how optimum weight varies according to role in physical activity and sport.

The requirements of a balanced diet

It is very important to eat a balanced diet, whether or not you take part in physical activity. The word diet refers to what you eat, although it is often used to suggest that someone needs to change his or her eating habits. You have probably heard other people say that they need to 'go on a diet', or make reference to specific diets such as low-fat or low-carbohydrate diets. 'Diet' in all of these cases is being used in a slightly different way. For the purposes of this course you need to think of diet as what you eat and a balanced diet as what you should eat.

Key word

Balanced diet – consuming all the different nutrients in the correct quantities

Actions

1. Write down all the things you think should be included in a balanced diet.
2. Make a note of the healthiest meal you have eaten this week.
3. Make a note of the unhealthiest meal you have eaten this week.
4. Compare your answers to a partner's answers – whose meals were healthiest?

A balanced diet is important as it will give you all of the nutrients you need to help you keep healthy and to provide the right amount of energy for the physical work that you do.

Current health studies show that a healthy balanced diet should contain:

- carbohydrates (starchy foods such as bread, potatoes, rice and pasta)
- fats (dairy products, fatty meat, sweets, biscuits and cakes)
- protein (found in meat, fish, eggs and beans)
- vitamins (mainly from fresh fruit and vegetables)
- minerals (found in most foods, particularly vegetables)
- water (found in most food and obviously liquids)
- fibre (found in vegetables, fruits, nuts and cereal).

Most people will eat a mixture of foods from these groups, but not necessarily in the correct proportions. Figure 16.1 shows the suggested ratio of these groups to achieve a balanced diet. (Water has not been included as it is not actually a food group.)

Key words

Macronutrient – nutrients that are required in large quantities in our diet: carbohydrates, fats and protein

Micronutrient – nutrients that are required in small quantities in our diet: vitamins and minerals

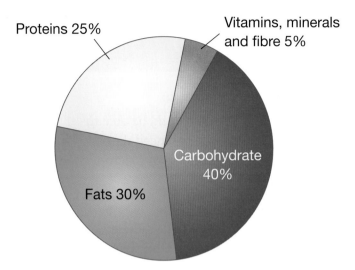

Proteins 25%

Vitamins, minerals and fibre 5%

Carbohydrate 40%

Fats 30%

Figure 16.1 Representation of macronutrients, micronutrients and fibre in a balanced diet for a healthy adult

Different texts will show slightly different percentages, but it is important to see from the different available sources of information that:

- all food groups are represented
- carbohydrates make up the bulk of our diet
- fats should not be removed from the diet.

Why we need these nutrients in our diet

Macronutrients

Carbohydrates are used to provide the body with energy for physical work. They can be used during aerobic or anaerobic activity.

Fats are used to provide the body with energy for physical work and to keep the body warm. They are used in aerobic activity.

Protein is generally used for growth and repair of new cells within the body, but can be used as an energy source in extreme circumstances (in other words, when usual energy sources are depleted). Protein is obviously very important to a sports performer as it is used in muscular hypertrophy (an effect of regular training, where the muscle increases in size).

Micronutrients

Vitamins and minerals are necessary because they help in the formation of the tissues of our body, such as hair, skin, nails, teeth and bones. They are also used in chemical reactions in the body to keep our body functioning and healthy.

Fibre is an essential aid to digestion. It is not digested by the body, but slowly makes its way through our digestive system before being expelled with other unwanted substances.

Water is essential in our diet, although it is not a nutrient. It prevents us from becoming dehydrated and helps to regulate body temperature. During periods of exercise we should make sure we drink more water than we do at rest to replace the water lost through sweating.

> **Check your understanding**
>
> 1. Name the three macronutrients we should have in a balanced diet.

How can sporting activity affect nutritional requirements?

The more physical work we do, the more energy we need to complete it. Food contains calories, which are used within the body to release energy for physical work. Sports performers will use more calories than those who do not exercise and so need to consume more food for energy. Performers must be careful, however, that they do not eat too much, otherwise excess carbohydrates will be stored as fat and provide additional weight. This will mean that they have to work harder every time they exercise because of the extra weight they are carrying. Athletes must ensure that Energy IN = Energy OUT.

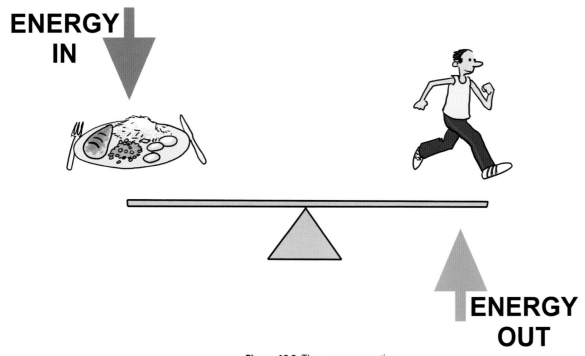

ENERGY IN

ENERGY OUT

Figure 16.2 The energy equation

In addition to eating the right amount of calories and correct ratio of nutrients, endurance athletes may use the process of carbohydrate loading to try to make sure they have the right amount of energy that can be made quickly available for their long events. If they are successful they will be able to continue to use carbohydrate as a fuel source rather than fat (see Chapter 5 for more detail).

Dietary manipulation

Carbohydrate loading

The aim of carbohydrate loading is to maximise carbohydrate stores prior to an endurance event. Remember, the body normally limits the amount of carbohydrate that can be stored, converting excess carbohydrate into fat stores. Carbohydrate loading is a method of dietary manipulation to try to get around this, to allow the performer to increase carbohydrate stores.

Key word

Taper – reducing the amount of something; in training this means reducing intensity of training prior to competition

The process involves 1 to 4 days of exercise taper (reducing the normal training load) while eating a high carbohydrate diet.

This combination of reduced training and increased carbohydrate intake results in increased stores of muscle glycogen (a form of carbohydrate that can be stored in the muscle).

This increase allows endurance athletes to exercise at their optimal pace for longer, improving times achieved by as much as 3%.

Timing of protein intake

Power athletes – those that work anaerobically – do not need the sustained supply of carbohydrates required by endurance athletes. Instead they need to focus on the timing of protein intake (when they should eat protein). During training or the activity itself, protein in the athlete's muscle will break down as a result of the work the athlete is doing. In order for the muscle to adequately repair after training, during rest and recovery, many athletes will immediately take in protein (for example, by eating a sports bar) to increase protein synthesis. The protein in the muscles is allowed to rebuild at a faster rate and therefore the muscles will be able to repair and grow.

Most people eat most of their protein with their evening meal. However, research suggests it would be better if our daily protein intake was balanced out across all three meals rather than leaving the bulk until the end of the day.

Actions

Make a note of the food you ate yesterday. How was your protein intake distributed throughout the day?

Figure 16.3 Different physical activities have different dietary requirements

Hydration levels

Water is an important part of the diet and becomes even more important when we exercise, as we need to compensate for the water lost through sweating (which we do to try to lose heat).

To perform well you need to make sure you are hydrated. This means drinking enough fluid before, during and after activity. A lack of water or dehydration could cause:

- fatigue
- muscle cramp

- dizziness
- nausea
- increased heart rate.

How much you have to drink during activity will depend on how hard you work (because this will impact on how much you sweat) and how hot or humid it is.

During the 2015 Virgin Money London Marathon more than 654,000 bottles of water were given out to the runners.

Figure 16.4 A player takes the opportunity to maintain hydration by drinking water

Figure 16.5 Fun runners in a marathon take the water from the volunteers

Hydration packs are a good way to carry water when you are participating in a long activity where access to water is difficult, such as when hill walking, mountain biking or skiing. The water is stored in a specially designed plastic sack. This is placed in a rucksack so that it can be worn, leaving the athletes hands free. A tube carries the water from the plastic sack to the athlete, like a large straw.

Check your understanding

2. Why is it acceptable for some people to eat more than others?

3. How would the following sports performers ensure they stayed hydrated during their events?
   - Cyclist
   - Marathon runner
   - Hill walker.

Key word

Optimum weight – the weight someone should be based on their sex, height, bone structure and muscle girth

Figure 16.6 You would not expect these two performers to weight the same!

Optimum weight

Guidelines are set by government health departments to indicate the weight range someone should fall within. These charts suggest whether someone is overweight or not by considering age, height and gender. They are based on averages and the assumption that if someone weights more than they should this is due to body fat. It is important to remember that these are only guidelines as optimum weight varies between individuals depending on the following factors.

Sex

There are differences in the structure and physiology of men's and women's bodies (you probably knew that!). On average, men have more muscle mass than women, although there are always exceptions. So even if a man and a woman were the same height, you would expect the man to weigh more than the woman due to the increased weight of his muscle. Because of this, men have an advantage over women in strength events, which is one of the reasons why men and women do not normally compete against each other in activities relying heavily on strength.

Height

The taller you are, the more you would be expected to weigh, therefore in some events it is helpful to be short because you will weigh less. For example, jockeys are normally very small and try to keep their weight as low as possible. Why do you think this would be an advantage in their event?

Bone structure

Some people have a bigger, denser bone structure than others and so will weigh more. This could be an advantage in contact sports where increased bone strength due to increased bone density is important to withstand physical contact.

Muscle girth

This is the size or circumference of the muscle. A larger circumference implies larger muscles, which explains why someone with large muscles may weigh more than the expected standard.

Being the 'correct weight' is important in most sports, but particularly important in the following activities:

- horse racing
- gymnastics
- boxing.

Do you know why?

Elite sports performers pay a lot of attention to their diet to make sure it is correct for their activity. The performers listed in Table 16.1 are all clearly the correct weight for their activities, but how does their weight compare with the 'expected' weight for their age and height using standard tables?

Actions

Look at the information in Table 16.1.

- Which performer is the lightest? What activity do they participate in?
- Consider the approximate weight and guideline weight for each of the performers. What do you notice? If the weight is more than that recommended, what might be causing the extra weight? If the weight is under that expected, why might this be the case?
- Can you see any link between weight and activity? Why are these performers considered to be the correct weight for what they do?
- What does this tell you about using standardised tables to judge whether you are overweight or underweight?

The recommendation for athletes is to ignore standardised charts to determine a healthy weight. This is because most of these athletes will be more muscular than non-athletes. As muscle mass weighs more than fat mass, muscular athletes will appear to have an unhealthy weight when in fact they are healthy and at a good weight for their activity.

Check your understanding

4. List the factors that can affect optimum weight.

5. Why will some people's bones weigh more than others?

PRACTICE QUESTIONS

1. Describe the requirements of a balanced meal.

2. Which nutrient should be eaten in the greatest quantities in a balanced diet?

3. Explain why protein is important to elite athletes.

4. Explain why all athletes do not use carbohydrate loading.

5. Explain why some elite performers in activities, such as rugby and sprinting, would be classed as overweight based on standard tables.

Study hints

Do not be tempted to abbreviate technical language in your examinations, for example, do not use the term carbs. Write the term in full – carbohydrates.

PERFORMER	HEIGHT	WEIGHT (AT TIME OF COMPETITION)	CLASSIFICATION USING STANDARD TABLES
Rugby – Greig Laidlaw	176 cm	80 kg	Overweight
Football – John Terry	187 cm	90 kg	Overweight
Jockey – Silvestre de Sousa	176 cm	50 kg	Underweight
Hammer throw – Alexander Smith	183 cm	115 kg	Obese

Table 16.1 Use of standard tables to determine a healthy weight can be misleading

Summary

- We should eat a balanced diet so we are healthy enough to exercise.
- The macronutrients needed in our diet are fats, carbohydrates and proteins.
- The micronutrients needed in our diet are vitamins and minerals.
- Sporting activity can affect our nutritional requirements.
- Carbohydrate loading increases muscle glycogen.
- Protein intake should be balanced across all three meals of the day.
- We need to make sure we stay hydrated during physical activity.
- Optimum weight is affected by sex, height, bone structure and muscle growth.
- Optimum weight varies according to role in physical activity and sport.

Useful websites

Reference intakes on food labels explained
http://www.nhs.uk/Livewell/Goodfood/Pages/reference-intakes-RI-guideline-daily-amounts-GDA.aspx

Athletes and protein intake
http://www.todaysdietitian.com/newarchives/060114p22.shtml

Healthy hydration guide
http://www.nutrition.org.uk/healthyliving/hydration/healthy-hydration-guide.html

Chapter 17 Classification of skills in physical activity and sport

Learning goals

By the end of this chapter you should be able to:

- classify a range of sports skills using the open–closed, basic (simple)–complex and low organisation–high organisation continua
- describe a range of practice structures and explain when they would be used
- apply knowledge of practice and skill classification to select relevant practice to develop a range of skills.

The skill continua

Different sports and physical activities require different skills. In order to perform well in a particular sport or physical activity we need to develop the skills required for that activity, for example, to play squash effectively performers need to have mastered the skill of serving, volleying, playing boasts and drop shots.

Actions

Look at the sports performers in Figure 17.1 and list the skills they are using in their sport.

(cont.)

Figure 17.1 Skill in sport and physical activity

In order for a coach to understand the best way to practice the range of skills needed to perform effectively in an activity, skills can be classified, those with similar demands being grouped together.

Three continua to classify skills are shown in Figure 17.2.

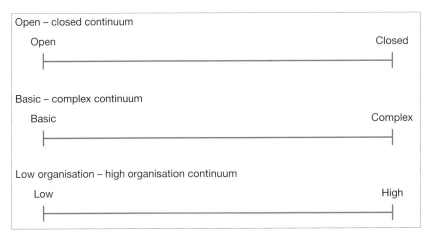

Figure 17.2 Skill continua

It is not always clear-cut exactly how a skill should be classified; this is why a continuum is used. As we can see in Figure 17.2 a continuum is represented by a straight line, drawn between two extremes.

Actions

The 'extremes' in Figure 17.2 link to skill. Can you think of five other pairs of extremes not related to skill? For example, Good–Evil.

A continuum allows for a better classification as we are able to show how close the skill, or whatever else is being classified, is to the extremes. Consider the extremes of Friendly–Unfriendly. How friendly are you? If you were friendly 100% of the time you would place yourself on the line at the extreme. However, if there are times when you are not friendly you would place yourself a bit closer to the unfriendly end of the continuum. The more unfriendly you are the closer you would place yourself to that end of the continuum.

Figure 17.3 Using a continuum

Actions

Look at the continua in Figure 17.4 What does this tell us about the characteristics of the person being classified?

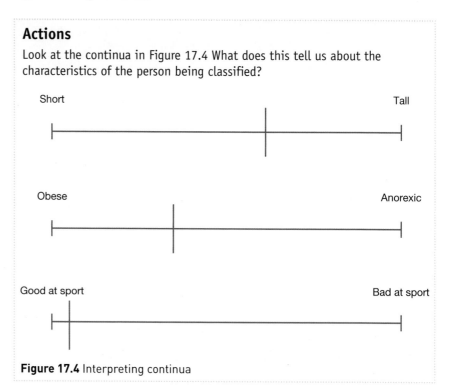

Figure 17.4 Interpreting continua

In the same way, we use continua to tell us more about a skill.

Actions

Think about the skills you use in one of your practical activities and answer the following questions:
- Is it as easy to perform the skills in competition as it is in practice? If not, why not?
- Is each skill as easy to perform? If not, what makes some skills harder than others?
- Was each skill as easy to learn? If not, why not?

The following points are some of the things you may have considered when answering these questions. Each numbered point relates to a different feature of a skill that will help to classify it:

1. It is easier to perform skills in practice because it is easier to control the situation, for example, in practice you don't have to worry about the opposition.

2. Not all skills are as easy to perform as some skills are more complex and require more thought to perform.

3. Some skills can be broken down into smaller parts, for example, a tennis serve. So if one aspect of the skill is faulty, for example, the ball toss, this can be focused on and practiced independently. By focusing on one part of the skill it is possible to improve the overall quality of the serve. Therefore, in this case, a difficult skill can be broken down making it easier to learn.

Open–closed continuum

The open–closed continuum relates to the environment in which the skill is performed. It is concerned with how much the environment can change when performing the skill. For example, if the skill is always performed in exactly the same conditions every time or not.

The environment can change due to:

- action of teammates, such as movement into a space so that a pass has to be hit harder, or with a change of direction to reach the intended target
- action of opposition, for example, if they try to intercept as you are about to make the pass you will need to adjust the pass to avoid interception.

A stable environment occurs when:

- performance of the skill is not really affected by the environment, such as when throwing the discus
- the skill is well-learnt or habitual (requires little conscious thought), for example, a gymnastics routine
- the performance of the skill is pre-planned, such as a set play in games.

Actions
Which of these two skills would be considered closed (to have the more stable, unchanging environment when the skill is performed)? Justify your answer.
- A gymnast performing a handstand.
- A badminton player playing an overhead clear during a rally.

Reconsider the skills in Figure 17.1, how many of these are closed skills?

Basic – complex continuum

The basic–complex continuum relates to the ease with which the performer can complete the skill, based on how much thought they need to give to the execution of the skill.

Key words

Open skill – a skill performed in a changing environment where the performer must react and adapt due to the actions of others, for example, a tackle in rugby

Closed skill – a skill performed in a stable, unchanging environment, for example, a gymnast completing a vault

Basic skill – a simple skill requiring basic movement patterns or little decision-making to execute, for example, running

Complex skill – a skill that requires a lot of thought and concentration before it is executed, for example, playing a through ball in hockey

A skill can be classified as basic if:

- it uses basic movement patterns, for example, running, swimming, cycling that can be performed with little conscious thought.
- it is well learnt so becomes habitual to the individual, for example, passing and receiving a ball.

A skill can be classified as complex if:

- the performer has to make decisions about how to perform it, for example, timing a pass to avoid the oncoming defender.

Key words

Low-organisation skill – a skill that can be broken down easily into smaller parts, for example, phases of the high jump

High-organisation skill – a skill that cannot be broken down easily into smaller parts, for example, a golf swing

Actions

Which of these two skills would be considered complex?

- A lay-up shot in basketball
- A 100 m sprint start

Reconsider the skills in Figure 17.1. How many of these would be classified as complex skills?

Low organisation–high organisation continuum

The low organisation–high organisation continuum relates to how easy it is to break the skill down into smaller parts to make the skill easier to practice.

Actions

Which of these two skills would be classified as a low organisation skill?

- A tennis serve
- A flick flack in gymnastics

Reconsider the skills in Figure 17.1. How many of these would be classified as high-organisation skills?

Actions

Copy and complete Table 17.1. Using one of your own practical 'team' activities think of three different skills and classify each by placing them on the continua.

Practical Activity:	Open–closed	Basic–complex	low-high organisation
Skill:	O C	B C	L H
Skill:	O C	B C	L H
Skill:	O C	B C	L H

Table 17.1 Classifying skills

Using an appropriate practice structure to improve skill

In order to improve our level of skill we need to practice. There are different ways to structure practice or training sessions depending on the skill or skills we wish to improve.

Actions

How might a training session be organised differently if you were structuring practice for an open rather than closed skill?

In a massed practice session there are little or no breaks. The performer will work on improving the same skill continuously.

Actions

Identify two advantages and two disadvantages of massed practice.

In a distributed practice session there are breaks, periods of time for recovery or opportunity to practice a different skill.

Actions

Identify two advantages and two disadvantages of distributed practice.

The advantages and disadvantages of these practice structures are given in Table 17.2.

Check your understanding

1. Identify and classify, using the open-closed, basic – complex, low organisation – high organisation continua, two contrasting skills that you use when playing in one of your individual practical activities.

2. Which type of skill would a player find easiest to perform, a complex or basic skill?

Key words

Massed practice – the repeated practice of a skill over a period of time without a break for recovery

Distributed practice – the repeated practice of a skill for a set amount of time with recovery periods, during which the performer may rest or engage in a different task

PRACTICE STRUCTURE	ADVANTAGE	DISADVANTAGE	CAN BE USED
Massed practice	1. Gives the performer plenty of time to focus on the skill they need to learn 2. Due to focus on one skill should mean that skill is developed quicker than if a range of skills were the focus	1. Performer will get tired without a break and so quality of performance will drop 2. The performer could get bored of repeating the same task all the time	When the performer is fit When the performer is motivated When learning a basic skill When learning a closed skill
Distributed practice	1. Reduces boredom/maintains motivation due to change in activity 2. Allows time for recovery, to receive feedback, or to mentally rehearse the skill 3. Develops ability to adapt skill to different situations due to different drills	1. May not give enough time to learn skill before moving on to another task 2. Must make sure that the change in activity within the session does not interfere with the learning of the previous skill, e.g. developing a smash in tennis and then changing to a smash in badminton	With beginners When skill is physically demanding or dangerous When learning complex skills When learning open skills

Table 17.2 Advantages and disadvantages of massed and distributed practice

Key words

Fixed practice – the repeated practice of a whole skill so that it becomes well learnt

Variable practice – a mixture of massed and distributed practice within a coaching session to allow changes of tasks so that the same skill can be repeated in different situations

In a fixed practice session, there is no attempt to break the skill down into smaller parts, therefore it is useful with basic skills that cannot be broken down or habitual closed skills.

In a variable practice session, a number of different drills or contexts can be given to practice a skill, such as shooting:

- into an empty goal
- in a 1 v 1 situation, for example, with a goal keeper present to defend the goal
- in a 2 v 1 situation with two defenders
- in a small, sided game.

Selecting a relevant practice structure for specific skill classifications

Table 17.3 summarises the practice structure that should be used for each skill classification. You need to be able to select the most appropriate practice structure to develop a skill. You also need to be able to justify your choice of practice structure.

PROBABLE PRACTICE STRUCTURE	SKILL CLASSIFICATION
Variable Distributed	Open Complex High organisation
Fixed Massed	Basic Closed Low organisation

Table 17.3 Matching practice structure to skill classification

Check your understanding

3. Identify the four different types of practice structures.
4. Describe the difference between massed and distributed practice.
5. Which type of practice would you use when teaching an open skill?

Actions

In your next practical session make a note of the practice structure used. Was it the most appropriate practice structure for the skill you were developing?

Actions

Devise a 30-minute training session to develop a relevant skill or skills for your sport. Consider the nature of the skill (how it is classified), the nature of the group (are they skilful, fit?) and therefore the best practice method to use.

PRACTICE QUESTIONS

1. Copy and complete the table to classify the golf swing using the stated skill continua.

Skill	Open–closed	Basic–complex	Low–high organisation
Golf swing			

PRACTICE QUESTIONS

2. Explain, using an example, why a complex skill is more difficult to execute than a simple or basic skill.

3. Explain why throwing the ball in for a line out in rugby could be considered a closed skill.

4. Describe variable practice.

5. Explain why you would teach a basic skill using massed practice.

Study hints
If a question asks for an example, make sure you provide one and that it is relevant to the question. In this case the example would be of a complex and basic skill.

Summary

- Sports skills can be classified using the open–closed, basic (simple) – complex and low organisation–high organisation continua.
- There are four types of practice structure:
  - massed
  - distributed
  - fixed
  - variable.
- Practice structure is selected based on the skill to be developed and the level of the performer.

Useful websites

Skills
www.bbc.co.uk/bitesize/higher/pe/skills_techniques/skills/revision/4/

Classification of motor skills: skill acquisition
https://www.youtube.com/watch?v=MyJzoXqfVx4

Types of practice
https://www.youtube.com/watch?v=6YWJ95bHjXU

Chapter 18 Goal setting

Learning goals

By the end of this chapter you should be able to:

- explain how goal setting can be used to improve performance
- describe the principles of SMART targets
- explain the value of each principle of SMART in improving performance
- apply knowledge of goal setting to set and review targets to improve performance.

Key words

Goal – an aim or task you set yourself; something you want to achieve

The use of goal setting to improve and/or optimise performance

Goal setting is an important skill to develop – if done properly it can help you in all aspects of your life. It can help you focus on what you want to achieve and give you small steps that ultimately allow you to achieve your overall goal or target.

GOAL-SETTING CAN:	
1.	increase attention/focus on what needs to be achieved
2.	increase motivation/effort (you work harder to achieve the 'goal')
3.	increase task persistence (helps you stick at something)
4.	allow you to assess progress over time (are you achieving your goals?)
5.	decrease stress (providing you set a manageable goal or target)
6.	lead to improved performance (due to the above points)

Table 18.1 Why goal-setting can improve performance

Check your understanding

1. Identify two ways goal setting can help to improve performance.

2. How can goal setting be used to decrease stress and anxiety?

Actions

The 6th point in Table 18.1 states that goal setting can lead to improved performance. Discuss, using examples, how each of the numbered points in Table 18.1 could help to improve or optimise your performance.

Principles of SMART targets and the value of each to improve and/or optimise performance

In order to be effective, goal setting needs to follow the principles of SMART target setting.

Each letter of SMART represents a principle that needs to be applied to any target or goal that is set. Different texts or websites may have slight variations on SMART target setting, but for your course any SMART target should be:

- **S**pecific
- **M**easurable
- **A**chievable
- **R**ealistic
- **T**ime-bound

Specific – goals need to be clear so that you know exactly what it is you are trying to achieve. A goal of 'getting better in my sport' is not specific. What aspects of the game or physical activity do you need to focus on to show improvement? Of these aspects, which will have the biggest impact on your performance?

Measurable – by setting measureable targets you will know if you have improved. You might have an initial goal to improve your sprint time; this becomes measurable by changing it slightly to 'improve my sprint time by one tenth of a second'. This is measurable because you can tell whether you are getting closer to the goal and when it is achieved, and can be motivating as you can see you are getting nearer to your target.

Achievable – this means you must only set goals or targets that you can accomplish, otherwise your motivation will drop because you know that the goal is not really attainable and therefore you are likely to give up. For example, a performer could set the specific and measurable goal to 'increase the height I can jump by 1 m'. This goal is not likely to be achievable (an increase of 1 m is surely too much?). Although the performer might try to increase the height jumped, inwardly they would know it was unlikely they would reach the target, at which point they may decide to give up.

Realistic – this principle works with the previous principle, achievable. Not only do you need to set achievable targets in terms of your ability, you also need to set targets that are attainable in terms of the resources required to fulfil the target. You need to make sure you have the time, money, opportunity and ability to fulfil any target. If you can, then the target will be realistic, otherwise the target will not be attainable and motivation to continue will be lost. The target also needs to be challenging to motivate you to work more to achieve it, but not so hard that you give up. This is why goals should really be discussed between the coach and the performer – the performer needs to feel that the goals are realistic if they are going to be prepared to work hard enough to achieve them.

Time-bound – goals need to have set dates by which they should be achieved. Without this it is too easy to keep putting off the goal: 'I will increase my training sessions from three to four a week' – but when? 'I will reduce my 100 m time by 100th of a second' – but when? In order to maintain the motivation to work hard to achieve the goal, clear deadlines have to be given. People will often have short-term goals leading to a long-term goal. For example, some athletes will have a long-term goal of competing in the 2020 Olympic Games in Japan; they will also have a series of short-term goals that will focus on aspects of their performance so they constantly improve leading up to the 2020 Olympics, so they get picked for Team GB and therefore achieve their long-term goal.

Key words

Specific goal – a clear, focused goal

Measureable goal – provides a way of checking to see if you have improved

Achievable goal – a task you know you can complete because you have the ability to do so

Realistic goal – a task you can complete because you have the resources to do so

Time-bound – a deadline to complete the task by

Actions

Copy and complete Table 18.2 by adding the relevant SMART principle(s) that could be applied to bring about the stated benefit. Justify your reasoning.

	Goal setting can:	Principle(s) of SMART Applied
1.	Increase attention/focus on what needs to be achieved	
2.	Increase motivation/effort	
3.	Increase task persistence	
4.	Allow you to assess progress over time	
5.	Decrease stress	

Table 18.2 Applying the SMART principles

Setting and reviewing targets

As part of your GCSE PE qualification you will need to plan, complete, analyse and evaluate a personal exercise programme (PEP), (see Chapter 24), for which you will need to:

- set appropriate SMART targets to improve your own performance
- justify your selection of SMART targets
- evaluate how effective you were in meeting your SMART targets.

When setting targets you must apply the SMART principles. Figure 18.1 includes a SMART target. Each aspect of the principles of SMART have been applied. The target is specific because we know exactly what the person aims to do. It is measurable as there is a time to achieve; we can see that it is achievable as they can currently complete the distance in 56 seconds, so they only wish to improve their time by 3 seconds over a 3-month period. It is realistic because they should be able to attain their goal based on their current ability and using the resources they currently use, for example, through training twice a week at the local pool. It is time-bound because there is a 3-month deadline to achieve the target in.

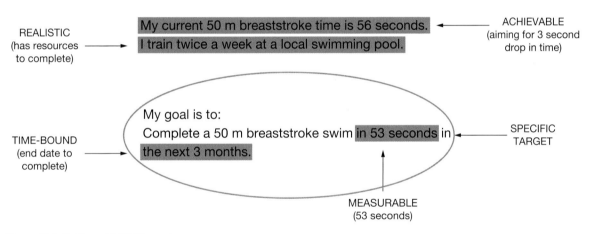

Figure 18.1 Setting a SMART target

Actions

Choose one of your practical activities where you most want to improve performance, or feel that improvement is most likely.

Using this activity and the principles of SMART target setting, set a fitness goal that could be used to bring about an improvement in your performance.

Create an image similar to that shown in Figure 18.1 to show where each principle of SMART is being addressed in your target.

Actions

How could you make the following target SMART?

Increase the average number of points scored in a basketball match.

Provided you set measurable targets, it will be possible to monitor progress. In order to set measurable targets you need to have something to measure. In some activities this is straightforward, for example, a 100 m sprinter would use time, but other activities appear less straightforward.

Actions

Identify the data that would be collected to monitor a performer's progress in the activities shown in Table 18.3. Use the sport's national governing body (NGB) website (see Useful websites box) if you are unsure how performance in that sport can be 'measured'. Think of a different example of data for each activity. Copy and complete the table.

Performer	Data collected
1500 m steeplechase	
Show jumping	
Gymnastic floor routine	
Pole vault	
Javelin	
Football	
Netball	
Basketball	

Table 18.3 Data that can be used to set measurable targets and to review progress against these targets

If you can monitor your progress, you can review it and use this to set new, or amend existing targets. Progress against targets should be reviewed regularly so that you know if:

- your performance is improving and getting closer to your goal (and therefore that your training is working)
- you have achieved your goal (and therefore need to think about what to do next)
- you need to amend an existing goal (because your current goal is no longer realistic, achievable, or provides the correct focus)
- you need to plan a new goal (because you have achieved your previous goal).

Check your understanding

4. State one reason why it is important to set measureable targets.

5. State two reasons why targets should be reviewed.

PRACTICE QUESTIONS

1. Explain, using an example, how the use of goal setting to increase focus on what needs to be achieved can improve performance.

2. Explain, using an example, how the use of a measureable target will help the performer know if their training programme is being effective.

3. What is an achievable goal?

4. Give an example of a suitable fitness goal for a squash player who loses any match where they have to play five games due to a lack in aerobic fitness.

5. Explain why the following is not a SMART target:

   My ability to avoid being tackled lets me down in matches, so I want to improve my ability to dodge defenders.

Summary

- Goal setting can be used to improve performance.
- Describe the principles of SMART targets.
- Explain the value of each principle of SMART in improving performance.
- Apply knowledge of goal setting to set and review targets to improve performance.

Useful websites

England Athletics
http://www.englandathletics.org/?hidesplash=1

British Equestrian Foundation
http://www.bef.co.uk/Detail.aspx?page=BEF

British Gymnastics
https://www.british-gymnastics.org

The Football Association
http://www.thefa.com/about-football-association

England Netball
http://www.englandnetball.co.uk

Basketball England
https://www.basketballengland.co.uk

Motivation and goal-setting for exercise
http://sportsmedicine.about.com/od/sportspsychology/a/motivation.htm

Olympic.org
http://www.olympic.org/content/olympic-athletes/athletes-space/tips/setting-smart-goals/

Learning goals

By the end of this chapter you should be able to:

- describe the use of visual, verbal, manual and mechanical guidance to optimise performance
- discuss the advantages and disadvantages of each type of guidance and evaluate their use in a variety of sporting contexts
- describe intrinsic, extrinsic, concurrent and terminal feedback and their use to optimise performance.

The use of visual, verbal, manual and mechanical guidance to optimise performance

Guidance is used as a way to help a performer learn a skill. There are four different types of guidance:

- visual
- verbal
- manual
- mechanical.

Each type of guidance can be used on its own, or in combination (for example, verbal guidance can be used with any of the other forms of guidance) to help a performer understand what they need to do to perform a skill or technique correctly. However, it is important that it is the right form of guidance and the right amount, so that the performer does not become 'overloaded' with information.

Actions

Discuss with someone else in the group what you think each type of guidance might involve and think of an example when it might be used.

Key word

Visual guidance – the use of a demonstration (or similar) to provide information to the performer to aid their learning of a skill

Visual guidance

This is when the performer is shown an image of the skill they need to perform. This image could be a picture of the movement, a set of pictures analysing the movement, showing each stage of the technique, a video or demonstration. The purpose of the image is to give the performer a mental picture of what they should be doing so they have something they can copy when they try the skill. It is essential that the demonstration is:

- accurate
- clear
- easy for the player to see
- repeated to allow the image to be remembered.

Otherwise, the performer will copy and therefore learn an incorrect technique.

Verbal guidance

This can be used independently but is often used with another form of guidance to reinforce the learning of the skill. The coach will use verbal guidance to describe a part of the skill, for example, a badminton coach may tell a performer to 'transfer your weight forward as you strike the shuttle'. If the performer is new to the skill this instruction will not make much sense on its own, therefore the badminton coach may demonstrate the skill and at the relevant point make reference to the need to transfer weight.

It is essential that verbal guidance is:

- accurate
- clear
- focused on the most important aspects of the skill.

Otherwise, the performer will become overloaded with information and will not be able to remember or focus on the most important parts of the skill and will therefore have difficulty learning the skill.

Manual guidance

This is provided by another person and will involve some type of physical support, such as supporting a gymnast in a handstand. It is used to help the performer get an accurate feel of the movement required to perform the skill or when the skill, if performed incorrectly, could cause injury. It is essential that manual guidance:

- allows the correct feel of the skill to be developed
- is not used so much that the performer becomes dependent on it.

Otherwise, the performer will learn the skill incorrectly, or never have the confidence to progress to attempt the skill without the use of the mechanical guidance.

Mechanical guidance

This is provided by an object. It provides a safe way to carry out a new skill, to develop an idea of how the movement should feel and, like manual guidance, is designed to reduce the risk of injury to the performer while they are learning a potentially dangerous skill. It is essential that manual guidance:

- allows the correct feel of the skill to be developed
- is not used so much that the performer becomes dependent on it.

Otherwise, the performer will learn the skill incorrectly, or never have the confidence to progress to attempt the skill without the use of the manual guidance.

Actions

Think about your last PE lesson, what types of guidance did your PE teacher use during the lesson?

Key words

Verbal guidance – this is the use of a verbal explanation from the coach to the performer about the correct way to complete a technique

Manual guidance – the performer is physically moved by the coach into the correct position to perform a technique to provide information about the feel of the movement

Mechanical guidance – the coach uses an aid to move the performer into the correct position when learning a skill, for example, a tumbling belt in gymnastics

Check your understanding

1. Identify the types of guidance being used in Figure 19.1.

Figure 19.1 Types of guidance

2. Why is it important that demonstrations are accurate?

3. Choose which you think is the example of mechanical guidance.

   A – Another archer giving clear instructions about how to position the body so the arrow hits the target

   B – A parent moving a player's arm through the correct action to play a tennis shot

   C – A coach using video playback so the player can see the required movement

   D – A swimmer using armbands or a float to prevent them drowning while practicing a swimming stroke

Evaluating the use of methods of guidance in a variety of sporting contexts

Before deciding on a type of guidance to use with a group or individual the coach should consider:

- the characteristics of the skill that needs to be mastered
- the ability level of the performer learning the skill
- the performer's safety.

Actions

Volunteer to assist in some PE or lunchtime sports sessions. During these sessions observe the teacher and make a note of the types of guidance they use during the session. Does the guidance they give vary depending on the activity they are taking? Does the guidance vary depending on the ability of the person being supported? Is the guidance effective?

Each of the methods of guidance have their own set of advantages and disadvantages. Clearly it is important for a coach to be able to evaluate when each type of guidance should be used and when it shouldn't.

Actions

Go through your notes and create a table that identifies two advantages and two disadvantages of each type of guidance.

Check your understanding

4. For each of the images in Figure 19.1 state why the coach will have used the type of guidance shown.

The use of intrinsic, extrinsic, concurrent and terminal feedback to optimise performance

Feedback is information given to a performer about the quality of their play. Feedback can be given:

- during the performance
- after the performance
- internally by the performer
- externally by someone else, for example, a coach.

The purpose of feedback is to aid learning, to help the performer correct errors in their technique or to correct mistakes made. It is also used to reinforce the correct action when a movement is performed well.

There is a range of types of feedback. You need to be aware of the following types:

- intrinsic
- extrinsic
- concurrent
- terminal.

Intrinsic feedback

There are sense organs within the body called proprioceptors that give the brain information about the position of the body, for example, our

Key word

Intrinsic feedback – information about the movement being carried out from the performers own body that can be used to detect errors and improve performance

arms or legs. The body will provide feedback that allows us to improve our skills, for example, in basketball when first learning to dribble the ball the player will use their eyes to collect information from 'outside' the body, looking to see where the ball is so they make correct contact with it. However, as they become more familiar with the skill they can use their proprioceptors to provide the required intrinsic feedback so they can continue to dribble the ball without the need to watch it.

Intrinsic feedback is valuable once a skill is well learnt, because the performer knows what the skill should feel like and can adjust their technique to get the correct feel, so they can detect and correct their own errors. As a beginner this is not possible because they will not have learnt the skill sufficiently well to be able to do this.

Actions

Try this: close your eyes and move your arms straight out to the side of your body. Keeping your eyes closed try to bring the index finger from each hand together – how close can you get without the fingers touching? What type of feedback are you receiving to allow you to do this?

Key words

Extrinsic feedback – information about the movement being carried out from external sources, for example, from a coach, in an attempt to improve performance

Concurrent feedback – information about the movement being carried out given at the same time that the skill is being performed

Terminal feedback – information given about a movement after it has been carried out

Extrinsic feedback

This is essential when a performer is first learning a skill because they will not be able to use intrinsic feedback. This information comes from outside of the movement, for example, from someone watching the movement, usually a teacher or coach, but could be from a peer or an observer. The feedback is normally verbal, telling the performer what was wrong with the skill and they will provide a relevant teaching or coaching point depending on the error.

Concurrent feedback

This is given while the performer is completing the skill. For example, a coach may give a coaching point during the movement. This helps the performer remember an important part of the technique that they normally forget. For example, reminding a discus thrower to wait as long as possible before bringing their arm through to increase the distance thrown.

Concurrent feedback can also be intrinsic. For example, if a skilful gymnast is running towards the vault they will know if they are travelling at the correct speed. They will know if their hands are placed correctly on the vault and if the body position they achieve is tucked enough to gain high marks.

Terminal feedback

This is given after the performance of the skill because it cannot be given during the movement. This might be because coaches are not allowed to coach during game play, for example, during tennis matches, or because the movement is over too quickly to provide feedback, for example, a front somersault on a trampoline. In both of these examples, of course, concurrent feedback could be provided intrinsically by the performer.

Figure 19.2 Use of intrinsic feedback when performing a skill

Factors affecting choice of feedback

There are a number of things the coach should consider before deciding on the best form of feedback to give. These include:

- the ability of the performer
- the type of skill being performed
- where the skill is being performed.

Ability of the performer

If the performer is skilful they:

- can rely more on intrinsic feedback, and be less reliant on the coach
- will be able to use feedback from the coach about tactics
- will be able to process concurrent feedback.

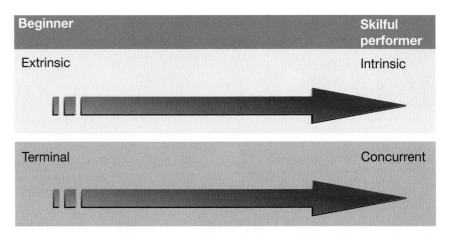

Figure 19.3 Use of feedback with different abilities of learner

Type of skill being performed

- If it is a complex skill it may be too difficult to give concurrent feedback.
- If it is a skill that is completed quickly it will be difficult to give concurrent feedback.

Where the skill is being performed

- If the skill is being performed during competition it might not be possible to give concurrent feedback.

Actions

Watch a live or recorded sports performance and identify when the coach or manager gives feedback – is it concurrent or terminal? Does it change from activity to activity?

PRACTICE QUESTIONS

1. Why should a coach, who is not good at demonstrating skills, ask a talented performer to demonstrate the skill to the group instead?

2. Explain why a coach would not use verbal guidance on its own with a beginner learning to play an overhead clear in badminton.

3. Explain two types of guidance you would use when teaching beginners to swim.

4. Describe the type of feedback you would use when teaching a canoeing group how to Eskimo roll in a swimming pool for the first time.

5. Explain why a coach may use terminal feedback when helping a performer correct errors in their technique.

Summary

- There are four different types of guidance:
  - visual
  - verbal
  - manual
  - mechanical.
- Guidance is used to optimise performance.
- Each type of guidance has different advantages and disadvantages making them suitable for different sporting situations.
- Intrinsic, extrinsic, concurrent and terminal are all types of feedback.
- The feedback given to a performer will vary depending on the situation and the performer's level of ability.

Useful websites

Revision – guidance techniques (pdf)
https://www.hoddereducation.co.uk/media/Documents/magazine-extras/PE%20Review/PE%20Rev%20Vol%20%208%20No%203/PERev-8_3-Guidance-techniques.pdf?ext=.pdf

Feedback in sport flipped
https://www.youtube.com/watch?v=V-cPCokSlHI

Chapter 20 Mental preparation for performance

Learning goals

By the end of this chapter you should be able to:

- describe how a warm up can be used for mental preparation
- describe mental rehearsal
- explain the benefits of mental preparation for performance.

Use of a warm-up for mental preparation

The purpose and importance of an effective warm-up has already been considered in Chapter 13. The purpose here is to focus on the opportunity for mental preparation during the warm-up. Mental preparation is considered equally important by elite sports performers. They need time to make sure they are psychologically prepared to perform at their best. Mental preparation allows them to take emotional control so they are confident in their ability to perform well. This makes sure that their actual performance does not suffer due to negative thoughts.

Actions

Have you ever been disappointed in your performance in physical activity, just felt that you didn't do as well as you could? List the reasons why you might not perform as well as you can in a competition. How many of these are down to psychological or emotional factors?

Check your understanding

1. Read the text in Figure 20.1. Which of the performers, Betsey or Alice, are more likely to perform at their best?

Betsey and Alice both take part in regular tennis competitions. Before the start of each competition both girls prepare by stretching and then using the practice courts to run through the shots they will need to play in the match, finishing off by practicing their serves. After their physical warm up the girls have a few minutes to wait until they can start the match.

During this time Alice focuses on the game ahead and how prepared she is, mentally going through her first serve and volley; she is focusing on her own performance.

While waiting for the match to start Betsey thinks about her opponent and wonders how good she is; she begins to worry that she will not be good enough to play her opponent.

Figure 20.1 Warming up before activity

Mental rehearsal

Coaches and performers use different techniques to help the performer form a 'mental picture' of the skill they need to produce. In Chapter 19 we saw that this mental picture is first formed through visual guidance and then reinforced through further guidance and feedback, until the performer has a very clear idea of what they should be doing in order to perform the skill correctly.

This 'mental picture' can then be used during breaks in training, for example, in distributed practice sessions during the recovery period. While the body is physically recovering the performer can mentally practice the skill.

Figure 20.2 Mentally preparing to compete in High Jump T42 event

Check your understanding

2. At what part of the warm up does mental preparation take place?

Key word

Mental rehearsal – forming a mental picture of a skill or technique you are about to perform

Actions

Think of elite athletes you have seen during their warm up. Think about how they go through the movement they are about to physically execute without actually doing the movement.

Actions

Copy and complete Table 20.1 giving an example of the skill, technique, event or tactic each performer may mentally rehearse during their warm-up.

Activity/performer	Could mentally rehearse
Rugby player	
Netballer	
Snowboarder in border cross	
100 m sprinter	
Relay runner	
Diver	
Triple jumper	

Table 20.1

Actions

Extend Table 20.1 with three more examples from different sports. What skills could you mentally rehearse for your practical activities?

Check your understanding

3. What does the term mental rehearsal mean?

4. Give an example of something a swimmer may mentally rehearse before a swimming race.

The benefits of mental preparation for performance

1. It can be used to learn a new skill.
2. It can be used to develop an existing skill.
3. It allows the performer to confirm what they need to do without having to do it and therefore saves energy for the event.
4. It can increase confidence in the performer that they will be able to successfully complete the skill.
5. It can help a performer concentrate.
6. Along with physical practice it can help improve performance.

PRACTICE QUESTIONS

1. Explain, using the information in Figure 20.1, why Alice is likely to have a better performance than Betsey.

2. Name the practice structure a coach should use to make sure the performer has time for mental rehearsal during their training sessions.

3. Describe what a long jumper may mentally rehearse.

4. Analyse the data in Figure 20.3 to determine the effect of mental rehearsal on performance.

5. Explain why a gymnast may perform better if they have mentally prepared for their activity.

Check your understanding

5. Identify two benefits of mental preparation for a performer.

Study hints

You are given two important bits of information to consider when answering this question: that you should use the information in the extract and that you should use it to justify why Alice will perform better. Make sure you use the information given in the question when answering.

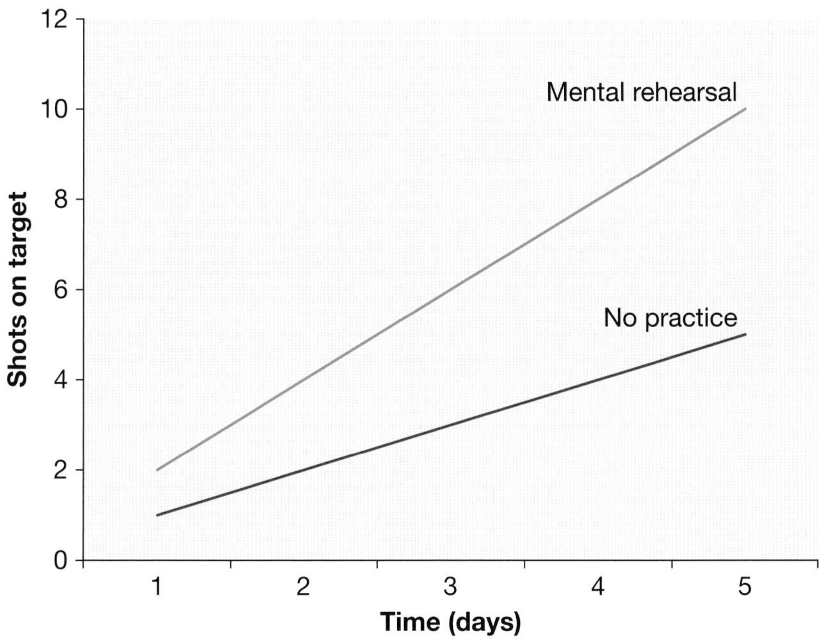

Figure 20.3 The effects of mental rehearsal on the performance of a target skill

Summary

- A warm-up should be used to physically and mentally prepare for performance.
- Mental rehearsal can be used to visualise the execution of a skill.
- Mental rehearsal can be used:
  - to learn a new skill
  - to develop an existing skill
  - as part of preparation for performance.

Useful websites

Mental rehearsal/visualisation/imagery
http://factorsaffectingperformance.weebly.com/mental-rehearsal.html

Visualisation key to improving sports performance
http://www.wholescience.net/2012/07/mental-rehearsal-key-to-improving-sports-performance/

Mental rehearsal/visualisation/imagery
https://sites.google.com/site/thepsychologicalgame/psychological-strategies-to-enhance-motivation-and-manage-anxiety/mental-rehearsalvisualisationimagery

Chapter 21 Participation in sport and physical activity

Learning goals

By the end of this chapter you should be able to:

- explain reasons for variation in participation rates based on personal factors of:
  - gender
  - age
  - socio-economic group
  - ethnicity
  - disability.
- analyse data associated with trends in participation rates.

Reasons for variation in participation rates based on personal factors

A consistent concern of past and present governments has been the health of the nation. As a result of this concern much money and resources have gone into researching ways to improve health. One of the clear messages from this research is that those people who exercise on a regular basis are at less risk of ill health than those that don't. Not surprisingly then the government monitors the levels of participation in sport and physical activity and looks for ways to increase participation rates in the hope that people will become healthier.

One of the roles of Sport England and the equivalent remaining home nation organisations is to help people develop a 'sporting habit for life', to develop grassroots sport. In order to see if their initiatives are working, Sport England collects data on an annual basis about participation in sport. This is Sport England's Active People Survey. The survey identifies how participation rates vary from place to place and between different sports and groups in society.

Sport England classify the different groups in society based on the following personal factors:

- gender
- age
- socio-economic group
- ethnicity
- disability.

Key words

Sport England – independent government organisation responsible for developing sport in England

Home nations – England, Scotland, Wales and Northern Ireland

Actions

Look at Figure 21.1 and discuss with a partner whether you think Sport England initiatives are working in increasing participation rates. Make a note of the points you make and feedback to the rest of the group.

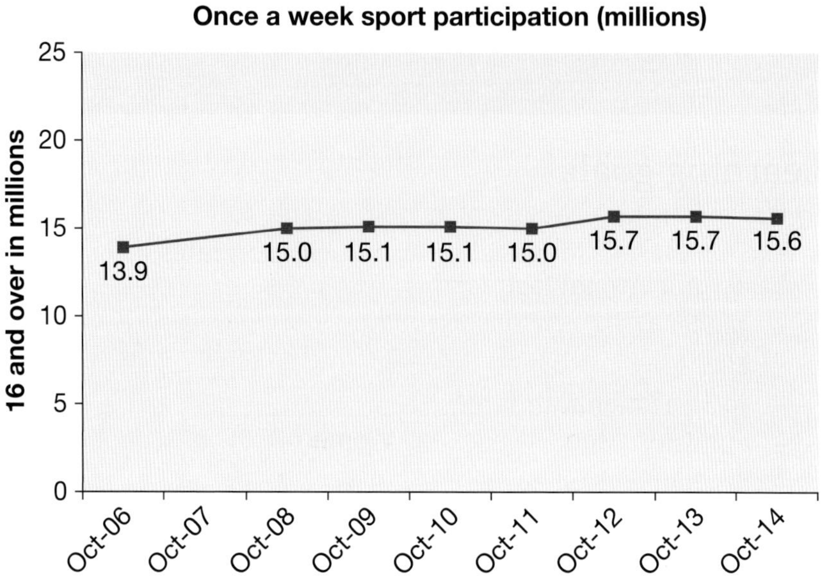

Figure 21.1 Weekly participations rates between 2006 and 2014
Source: Sport England Active People Survey 8 October 2013 – October 2014

So what makes us want to get involved in physical activity? OK, we know that it is 'good' for us physically, emotionally and socially, but so are a lot of other things that we don't necessarily want to do: revision, early nights, not eating junk food, not smoking. Yet many people still do these things. So what actually influences whether we take up physical activity or not, and if we do, the activities we do? For example, if you play football, why do you play this rather than golf (or vice versa)?

Actions

1. Make a list of all the physical activities you are involved in. List all of the activities on the board for the group, keeping a tally of how many times a specific activity is mentioned.
2. Look at the list you have compiled for Action 1.
   - Do the same number of people play each activity?
   - If not, what activities are more popular?
   - Why are these activities played more?
   - Why are some activities participated in less?

It might help if you think about why you started playing the activities you did.

3. Go back to the list on the board of all the activities that your group participates in. Extend the list to include the activities your family and friends play.
4. If you have added any extra activities to your list:
   - What is different about the added activities?
   - Are there any reasons why they were not on the list that you and the rest of the group participate in?
5. What activities are missing?
   - Make a list of any other activities you can think of that are not listed already.
   - Why don't you do any of these activities?

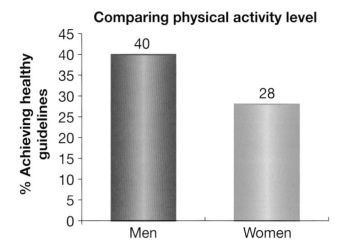

Figure 21.2 Comparing physical activity level between men and women
Source: Health Survey for England, 1998

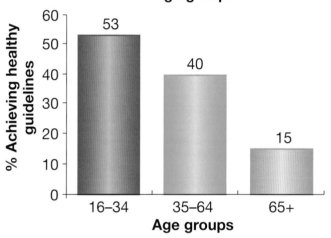

Figure 21.3 Comparing physical activity level between age groups
Source: Health Survey for England, 2007

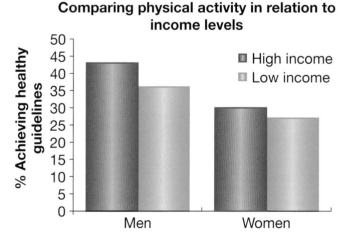

Figure 21.4 Comparing physical activity level in relation to income
Source: Health Survey for England, 2007

Hopefully you are starting to build a list of the factors that can influence your choice of physical activity. Check your ideas against those given in Tables 21.1 and 21.2.

Actions

Look at Figures 21.2, 21.3 and 21.4. What seems to be influencing the amount of practical activity in these figures?

	PERCENTAGES
Health isn't good enough	47.0
Not really interested	18.4
It's difficult to find the time	18.2
I am too old	2.7
It costs too much	2.1
I wouldn't enjoy it	1.8
Never occurred to me	1.6
No one to do it with	1.1
I am too lazy	1.1
Other reasons	5.9

Table 21.1 Main reasons for non-participation in physical activity
Source: Taking Part Survey, 'Taking Part: The National Survey of Culture, Leisure and Sport', The Department for Culture, Media and Sport

	PERCENTAGES
Less busy	39.3
Cheaper admission process	11.0
People to go with	8.7
If I had more free time	6.4
Better playing facilities	3.5
Improved transport/access/more cycle lanes	3.2
Help with childcare/crèche facilities	3.1
If there were more/better variety of local facilities	3.0
Better facilities, e.g. cafes, changing rooms	2.8
Longer opening hours	2.7
If the weather was better	2.5
If I had better health	1.7
Better equipment	1.6
Support for my specific needs, e.g. injury or disability	1.3
Safer neighbourhood	1.2
Better information on what to do	1.0
If I had more motivation/more energy	1.0
Other reasons	5.8

Table 21.2 Factors that would increase participation
Source: Taking Part Survey, 'Taking Part: The National Survey of Culture, Leisure and Sport', The Department for Culture, Media and Sport

Some of the reasons given in Table 21.1 for not participating seem to be related to lack of motivation/fun/enjoyment. For example, 'Not really interested', 'Never really occurred to me', 'I wouldn't enjoy it', 'I am too lazy'. If this were your attitude how might it change if your friends all took part in the activity? Would you be more motivated because you knew they were going? Would you have fun because your friends were there? Would it motivate you to be more energetic even if you felt lazy? If so, then people can influence your choice of whether to be active or not and also the activity you participate in.

Check your understanding

1. Using Figure 21.1 identify:
   - the age group that the data is focusing on
   - the scale used in the graph
   - the number of participants in Oct-11.

The personal factors impacting on participation you need to be aware of for your examination will now be discussed.

Personal factors and why they might impact on participation

Gender

Although more activities are becoming recognisable as suitable for both sexes, there is still gender bias associated with some sports. This means that while men and women may participate in sport, they may only choose activities that they believe are socially acceptable.

Actions

1. Look at the activities listed in Table 21.3.
2. Copy and complete Table 21.3 by placing a tick to indicate the gender associated with each sport.

Activity	Male	Female
Badminton		
Rugby		
Netball		
Football		
Dance		
Gymnastics		
Diving		
Boxing		
Aerobics		

Table 21.3 Gender based activities?

3. Compare your answers with others answers. Were they the same? Why did you make the selections you did? Shouldn't it be possible for both genders to participate in whatever sport they want?

Actions

Look at the two images of successful sports women in Figure 21.5. Is either activity more acceptable than the other?

Figure 21.5 Are some sports still more socially acceptable?

Age

Why might the activity you choose vary with age? Look at Table 21.4. Which age group do you associate with each activity? Explain your choice.

Copy and complete the table.

ACTIVITY	ASSOCIATED AGE GROUP: YOUNG/OLD/ANYONE	REASON FOR CHOICE
Football		
Cricket		
Badminton		
Crown green bowls		
Rambling		
Horse riding		
Skiing		
Snowboarding		

Table 21.4 Physical activity and age

The competitors in Figure 21.6 are 104 and 95 – the pictures were taken when they were competing for their country.

Figure 21.6 Going against the stereotype

Socio-economic group

Choice of activities will vary depending on the following:

- **Cost** – some activities are more expensive than others due to playing fees (hire of court, for example), cost of equipment or travel to venue. Those people with a limited amount of disposable income (not much cash) will not have as big a choice of activities as those with more money.

- **Status** – some activities are associated with different socio-economic groups within society.

- **Socio-economic group** is often associated with the amount of personal wealth; this is because it is a classification of people's occupation. Different levels of occupation earn more money, traditionally the more responsibility you have the more your wages increase. Those with a 'higher occupation' or socio-economic group, such as high managerial or professional occupations, will earn more. Those with limited responsibility in an intermediate or 'lower' socio-economic occupation or group will earn less. For example, a teacher will earn more than a supervisor on a shop floor.

Key word

Socio-economic group – a way of classifying people by their occupation. For example, managerial or lower supervisory

Look at Table 21.5. Who do you associate with the activities? Copy and complete the table.

ACTIVITY	SOCIO-ECONOMIC GROUP ASSOCIATED WITH ACTIVITY. HIGHER OR LOWER?	REASONS FOR CHOICE
Cricket		
Football		
Rugby		
Boxing		
Rowing		
Athletics		
Polo		
Tennis		

Table 21.5 Physical activity and socio-economic group

Key word

Stereotypes – these are commonly held, oversimplified, preconceived ideas about a person or group. They can be positive or negative

Ethnicity

In the way that women and men are still associated with some sports, the same applies to ethnicity. There are no physical reasons why one group of people should be inherently better at one activity than another, but due to stereotyping some people believe that different ethnic groups are better at different sports. Because of this, people from different ethnicities are often encouraged (through the media and significant others) into particular sports.

Actions

Look at Table 21.6. What ethnicity do you associate with each activity? Copy and complete the table by placing a tick to indicate the ethnicity associated with each sport. Remember you are dealing with stereotypes – it is up to you and your class to try to break some of these stereotypes!

Activity	Asian	Asian British	Black	Black British	White	Any
Athletics – sprinting						
Cricket						
Badminton						
Boxing						
Athletics – long distance						
Horse riding						
Men's hockey						
Tennis						

Table 21.6 Activities based on ethnicity?

Disability

Clearly, if you have a disability it may limit how you participate in an activity, although given the right resources most sports can be adapted (see Figure 21.7).

Barriers

The personal factors listed above do impact on participation rates, but why? Why should gender make a difference? Why should your ethnicity make a difference? In addition to stereotyping there are other reasons why certain groups may not participate as much as others. These tend to be due to the following barriers:

- **Access** – facilities might exist, but there might be age restrictions preventing access. Similarly, if the facility is a bus ride away, or not accessible by public transport, you still cannot get to the facility.

Figure 21.7 Physical activity and disability

- **Availability** – you might be restricted due to the facility's opening hours or the times that classes for juniors or beginners are available. For example, if you wanted to take up a new sport and beginners' taster sessions were on Saturdays but you had a part-time job on a Saturday, you could not go and so would be unlikely to take up the activity. Availability also relates to finding appropriate venues – if you cannot find a club to play at, you won't be able to play. For example, you might like to try skiing, but if you don't live near a mountain or an artificial ski slope, it will be very difficult to get involved in this physical activity.

- **Time** – a lot of people say they would participate in something if only they had the time to do so.

- **Money** – some activities are more expensive than others, thus denying you access to them (for example, a golf club would be a lot more expensive than a council-owned facility, so although the facility existed you still could not access it).

- **Health problems** – some health problems will prevent participation in some types of activities and so limit the person's choice. This does NOT mean, however, that all physical activity needs to stop. People with health problems should consult their GP to establish an appropriate level of physical activity.

Study hints

Wording of questions is very important. Here the emphasis is on the overall trend so you will need to look at the starting point and the end point. Does it finish higher, lower, has it stayed the same?

Check your understanding

2. Using Figure 21.2, who participates more – men or women?

3. Using Figure 21.3, which age group is the most active?

4. Using Figure 21.4, which group has the lowest level of participation?

5. Apart from stereotyping, what other barriers are there to participation?

PRACTICE QUESTIONS

1. Using Figure 21.1, state the overall trend in participation rates. Justify your answer.

2. Analyse Figure 21.1 to determine the changing patterns in participation rates between 2006 and 2014.

3. Analyse Figure 21.3 to determine the impact of two personal factors on participation rates.

4. Figure 21.8 shows participation rates for different groups in England. Analyse Figure 21.8 to determine the three personal factors most likely to influence participation in physical activity.

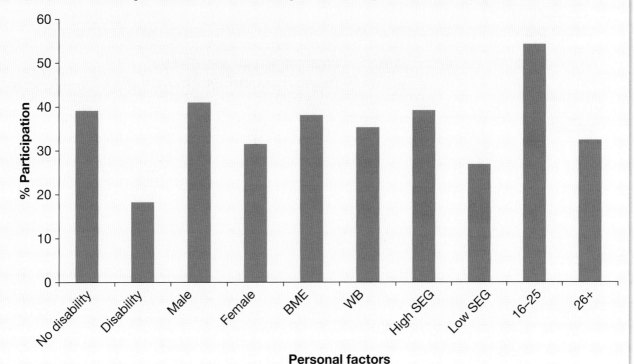

Figure 21.8 The impact of personal factors on participation rates

Key – BME Black and minority ethnic groups; WB White British; SEG Socio-economic group

PRACTICE QUESTIONS

5. Figure 21.9 shows participation rates in physical activity and sport. Analyse Figure 21.9 to determine the trend in participation in these activities.

Participation rates by sport

Once a week participation (16+), England. Percentage change since October 2010–11

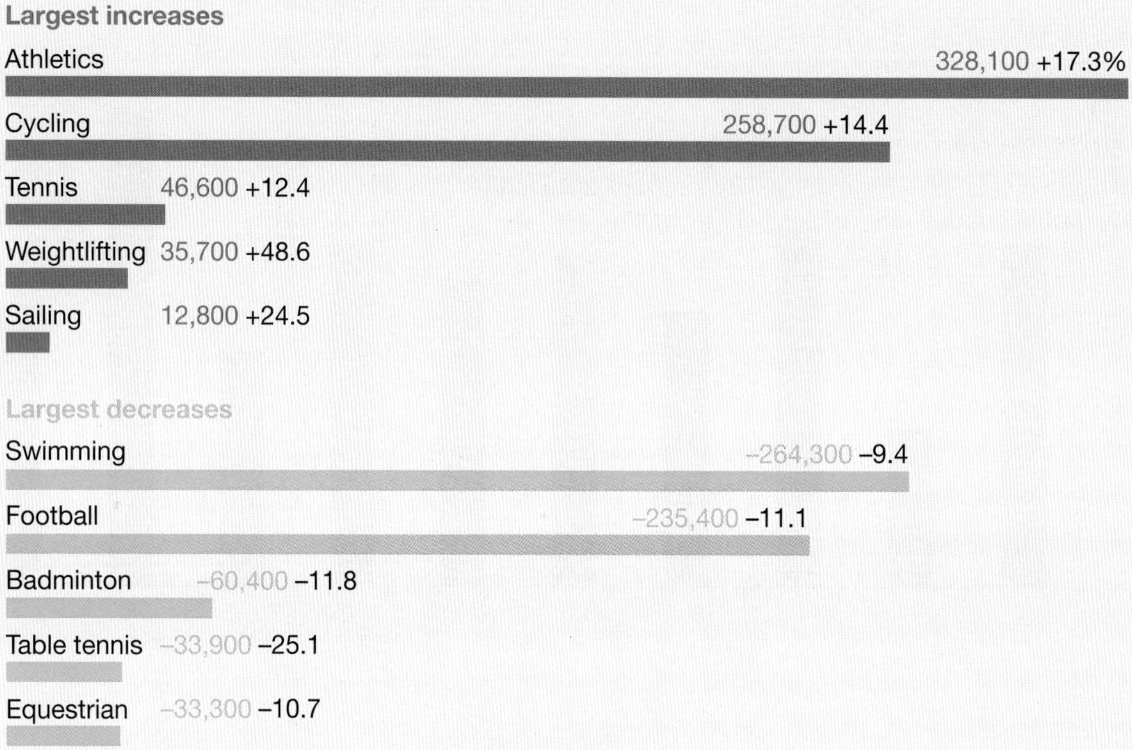

Largest increases

Athletics   328,100 +17.3%

Cycling   258,700 +14.4

Tennis   46,600 +12.4

Weightlifting   35,700 +48.6

Sailing   12,800 +24.5

Largest decreases

Swimming   −264,300 −9.4

Football   −235,400 −11.1

Badminton   −60,400 −11.8

Table tennis   −33,900 −25.1

Equestrian   −33,300 −10.7

Source: Sport England

Figure 21.9 Participation rates by sport

Summary

- Participation rates in physical activity and sport vary among different social groups
- The personal factors that impact on participation rates are:
  - gender
  - age
  - socio-economic group
  - ethnicity
  - disability.
- Different groups face different barriers to participation.
- Barriers to participation are:
  - access
  - availability
  - time
  - money
  - health.

Useful websites

Sport England – The national picture
http://www.sportengland.org/research/who-plays-sport/national-picture/

National governing bodies of sport
http://www.efds.co.uk/our_work_in_sport/national_governing_bodies_ngbs_of_sport

Women's Sport Trust
http://www.womenssporttrust.com

Sporting Equals
http://www.sportingequals.org.uk

British Heart Foundation – Physical activity statistics 2015 (pdf)
https://www.bhf.org.uk/~/media/files/publications/research/bhf_physical-activity-statistics-2015feb.pdf

Learning goals

By the end of this chapter you should be able to:

- describe the relationship between commercialisation, the media and physical activity and sport
- discuss the advantages and disadvantages of commercialisation and the media for
  - the sponsor
  - the sport
  - the player/performer
  - the spectator
- analyse data associated with trends in the commercialisation of physical activity and sport.

Commercialisation, the media and sport

Key words

Commercialisation – making a product available for purchase

Sponsorship – cash or resources paid for a commercial return through increased exposure of a brand

Actions

1. Look at Figure 22.1.
2. What is the sports performer advertising?
3. Compare your list with others in the group
4. Analyse the list of sponsors. Is there any commonality between brands? Is there a clear target audience?

Figure 22.1 Commercialisation and sport

Actions

Look at Figure 22.2. What types of sponsorship companies are represented? What do they hope to gain from sponsoring the Olympics? What did it cost them? Do you think all of the sponsors are an appropriate choice to be advertised at a major international sports event?

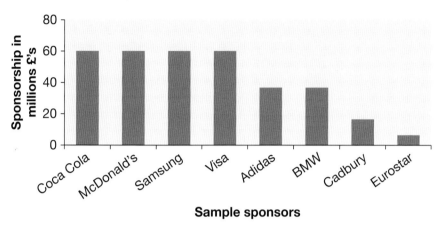

Figure 22.2 A few of the sponsors for the London 2012 Olympics

Actions

Go through your textbook and look at images of other performers. How much advertising do you see in these images? Is there a difference between activity or level of activity?

You will have seen many examples of sponsorship in sport as a form of commercialisation. Companies pay sports organisations/associations or sports performers to wear their brand or display the name of the brand when they are performing. Some of these brands have nothing to do with sport.

Actions

Watch a sporting event on the television and copy and complete Table 22.1 by identifying the sport- and non-sport-related products being advertised.

Sport-related product	Non-sport-related product

Table 22.1 Products that are promoted through sport

But why are companies prepared to pay millions of pounds to have their product seen? What's in it for them?

- Commercialisation is about selling a product – through increased awareness of a product more people are likely to buy it therefore the company hope that they will earn more in increased sales than the cost of the sponsorship.

Do you think all sports receive the same amount of sponsorship? If not, which sports would receive more? Why?

- Manchester United's 7-year sponsorship deal (2015–2022) with Chevy is worth $560 million and a $1.4 billion deal with Adidas from 2016.
- Rory McIlroy, golfer, has a 10-year sponsorship deal with Nike worth $250 million.

If commercialisation is all about selling more products, then it stands to reason that those sports with the highest profile will receive more sponsorship. This is where the link to the media is made. People use the media to follow the success of their teams, whether this is reading about them in the paper, listening on the radio or watching via the television or internet. The more popular a sport the more the media will cover it.

Actions

1. Look at the weekly television schedule – how much sport is on the television? Are all sports represented? If not, why not?
2. Look at Table 22.2. Note the difference in the number of major events that are broadcast in a year. Some of these events will involve multiple matches, for example, two of the televised football events are the Premier league: this has 116 televised games, or the Football league that has 112 televised games. With the increased exposure to the public it is no wonder that football attracts such large sponsorship deals.

Sport	Number of televised events	Provider (Terrestrial, e.g. BBC and ITV or Satellite, e.g. Sky and BT Sports)
Football e.g. the premier league (116 games) or UEFA Champions League (12 games) = 2 televised events	58	Both
Athletics e.g. IAAF World Championships in Athletics or Great North Run	35	Both
Cycling	19	Both
Disability sports	10	Both
American football	7	Satellite
Ice hockey	4	Satellite
Gymnastics	3	Terrestrial
Netball	3	Satellite
Badminton	1	Sky

Table 22.2 Sports broadcasting contracts in the UK

Source: https://en.wikipedia.org/wiki/Sports_broadcasting_contracts_in_the_United_Kingdom

For your second written exam you need to be aware of the relationship between commercialism, the media and sport. This is often illustrated through 'the golden triangle'. The golden triangle is a representation of money making within sport.

Golden Triangle

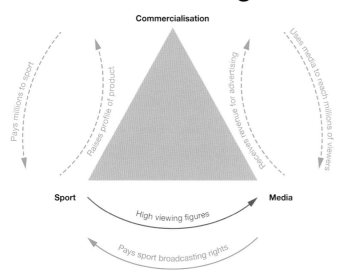

Figure 22.3 The golden triangle

The advantages and disadvantages of commercialism and the media in sport

Some of the advantages and disadvantages of the relationship between commercialism, the media and sport are shown below:

For the **sponsor**

- increased awareness of brand therefore more products sold so increased profit
- associated with performer who has poor reputation could have negative impact on product sales, for example, drug use, illegal activity outside of sport.

For the **sport**

- increased income
- money from broadcasting means clubs are less reliant on ticket sales at fixtures
- use of income to buy better players
- better facilities
- better training resources
- less control over sport (for example, timing of matches)
- format of sport can change to make it more exciting for television viewers, for example, 'golden goals'.

For the **player/performer**

- global superstars
- earn vast sums of money
- in public eye/reduction in private life
- become a commodity that can be bought and sold

Check your understanding

1. Using Figure 22.2, work out what was the highest amount of sponsorship from any one company in the 2012 Olympics.

2. Using Figure 22.2 give an example of a sponsor whose product relates to sport.

3. Give an example of a product sponsored by sport that is not sport-related.

- increased risk of injury due to extended length of playing season
- increased pressure to 'perform' to maintain sponsorship
- may become associated with a negative product.

For the **spectator**

- more exciting players to watch
- better facilities
- more competitions
- more opportunity to watch sport
- sports played at a time they are more likely to be able to watch
- some sports only accessible via satellite TV or 'pay per view' therefore increased cost.

Actions

Research rule changes in popular televised sports and report your finding back to the rest of the class.

Compare your finding to the examples in Table 22.3.

Rule change	Effect
Twenty20 cricket	Game created to increase the pace of the more traditional game to increase spectators
Golden goal in football	Used to decide the winner of a knockout round in a competition if scores are equal at full time. Provides a quick conclusion to the match and makes it exciting for viewers
Badminton	A change to the American scoring system of a point per rally to make the game more exciting to watch
Glass courts in squash	To make the sport easier to televise

Table 22.3 Examples of changes to sport to make the sport more entertaining

Actions

All of the performers in Table 22.4 lost their sponsorship as a result of behaviour that reflected badly not only on the individual but the sponsor. As a result each athlete lost their sponsorship deal worth millions of pounds. Discuss why you think the sponsor did not want their product or brand name associated with the performers?

Performer and sport	Sponsor	Action
Lance Armstrong (cycling)	Nike	Taking performance-enhancing drugs
Barry Bonds (baseball)	Mastercard, KFC	Taking performance-enhancing drugs
Adrian Peterson (American football)	Castrol oil, Nike	Child abuse
Ray Rice (American football)	Nike	Spousal abuse
Wayne Rooney (football)	Tiger beer	Infidelity
Mike Tyson (boxing)	Pepsi	Spousal abuse
Tiger Woods (golf)	Gillette, Gatorade, Tag Heuer	Infidelity

Table 22.4

Actions

Look at Table 22.5 and discuss whether you think these are appropriate sponsors for sport.

Sponsor	Sport
Coral (betting)	Football
Mitre (sports equipment)	Football League
Herbalife (sports nutrition)	Cristiano Ronaldo
BMW	Berlin Marathon
Coca cola	Olympic Games
McDonald's	Olympic games
Chang (Thai beer)	Football

Table 22.5 Sports sponsorship

Study hints

If you are given data in a question, make sure you look at all of the data so that you understand the message it is presenting.

PRACTICE QUESTIONS

1. Copy and complete Table 22.6 identifying three sports-related brands and three non-sports-related brands being advertised in Figure 22.4.

Sports related brands	Non-sport related brands

Table 22.6

Figure 22.4 Advertising in winter sports

2. Analyse Figure 22.5 to determine
   (a) which team receives the greatest amount of sponsorship
   (b) the teams who have sponsorship deals for their stadium and jersey
   (c) the greatest amount of sponsorship for a jersey.

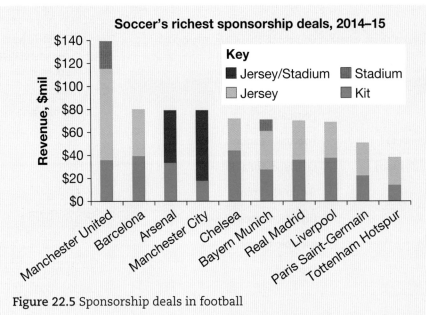

Figure 22.5 Sponsorship deals in football

3. Using Table 22.2 explain why netball is unlikely to receive much sponsorship.

4. Using Table 22.2 explain why the media seems more interested in broadcasting football than any other sporting event.

5. Justin Gatlin is an elite American sprinter. Despite serving two bans for taking performance-enhancing drugs, his sponsorship deal with Nike was renewed.

State one reason why Nike:

   (a) should have renewed Justin Gatlin's sponsorship
   (b) should not have renewed Justin Gatlin's sponsorship.

Summary

- Commercialisation, the media and physical activity and sport rely on each other for their success.
- Companies are prepared to pay large sums of money to sponsor sport or elite sports performers.
- Sport and elite sports performers are used to advertise products.
- The media increases ratings by reporting on sport.
- The increase in funding for sport through sponsorship can lead to improvements for spectators.
- There are disadvantages of sponsorship.

Useful websites

AS socio-cultural golden triangle
https://www.youtube.com/watch?v=6_DZvcvYdJg&app=desktop

The global sports media consumption report 2014 (pdf)
http://www.knowthefan.com/wp-content/uploads/2014/05/KTF_GlobalOverview_2014_WEB.pdf

Women in sport – stats pack
https://www.womeninsport.org/wp-content/uploads/2015/04/Media-Stats-Pack-June-2015.pdf

Chapter 23 Ethical and socio-cultural issues in physical activity and sport

Learning goals

By the end of this chapter you should be able to:

- explain the different types of sporting behaviour: sportsmanship, gamesmanship
- give examples of types of deviance at elite levels of sport
- explain the reasons for, and consequences of, deviance at elite level.

Sportsmanship and gamesmanship in physical activity and sport

Are you a 'good sport'? Do you congratulate your opponent when they play a good shot or if they win? Do you own up if you break the rules but the referee doesn't see? Do you always play by the rules? Are you prepared to be fair to your opponent, for example, acknowledging if you hit the ball off of the pitch? If you answered yes to all of these questions you sound like a good sport, someone who displays sportsmanship.

Unfortunately, there is still plenty of evidence of gamesmanship in elite level sport. Some players will look for an unfair advantage over their opponents, while still keeping within the rules of the sport. These players will push the boundaries of the rules as far as they will go without actually breaking them. For example, time wasting if you have a lead and want to minimise your opponent's chance of equalising.

National governing bodies (NGBs) try to encourage fair play and sportsmanship in their players as it:

- encourages players to behave in an appropriate sporting manner on the field of play
- provides good role models for grassroots players so they are more likely to copy good behaviour
- puts the sport in a good light
- makes the game more exciting as fewer stoppages, for example, if timewasting or diving
- gives a more accurate result – the best team win
- makes the game safer, performers are less likely to get injured, for example, an 'elbow' in an off the ball incident
- helps maintain player health, for example, the negative side effects of performance-enhancing drugs.

The NGBs encourage fair play through:

- rewards
- awards
- punishment.

Key words

Sportsmanship – qualities of fairness, following the rules, being gracious in defeat or victory

Gamesmanship – bending the rules/laws of a sport without actually breaking them

Sledging – a term used in cricket when players try to gain an advantage by insulting the opposition

Deviancy – doing something against the norms or values of society

Actions

Can you name three elite performers who you think display sportsmanship?

Actions

Read the case study in Figure 23.1. Would you have been prepared to do the same for your opponent?

Figure 23.1 Sportsmanship at elite level of sport

Martin Damsbo

Denmark, Archer

Awarded Fair Play Trophy for Act of Fair Play

Individual Bronze Medal Final of the Archery World Cup, Stage 2, in Antalya, Turkey.

The bronze medal match was between Martin Damsbo (Denmark) and Braden Gellenthien (USA). Both were warming up on the practice range before their match when Braden's bow malfunctioned and could not be repaired in time for the final. Braden could not use his spare bow, either, as that had also malfunctioned earlier that day and could not be repaired sufficiently for the final.

For an archery match, athletes are required to have two bows as there is not time out for equipment failure, should one of the bows malfunction during the match. With no hesitation, Martin offered Braden his spare bow, so that Braden could compete in the match. Although Martin won the match in the end, WA wishes to nominate Martin for his unconditional generosity and sportsmanship that made him lend his spare equipment to an opponent, without taking into account the medal, the prize money and the ranking points at stake for the qualification for the end of season World Cup final in Paris.

Source: http://www.fairplayinternational.org/world-fair-play-awards-for-the-year-2013

Actions

Look at the list of actions in Table 23.1 that players may engage in. Place a 'tick' in the relevant column if this is sportsmanship, gamesmanship or outside of the rules of the game. Copy the table and complete by adding three more examples from one of your activities.

Action	Sportsmanship	Gamesmanship	Against the rules
Shaking hands and congratulating opponent at the end of a tennis match even though you lost			
Sledging in cricket			
Diving in football			
Kicking the ball out of play if an opponent is injured			
Clapping an opponent in volleyball when they have made an error			
Helping an opponent up from the floor if they have fallen			

Table 23.1 Examples of gamesmanship and sportsmanship in sport

Actions

Look at the names of the sports performers in Table 23.2.

How would you group these players? Who displays sportsmanship when they play? Do any display gamesmanship?

David Beckham	Steve Redgrave
Diego Costa	Luis Suarez
Giles Scott	Sachin Tendulkar
Cristiano Ronaldo	Lionel Messi
Usain Bolt	Kobe Bryant
Roger Federer	Rory McIlroy

Table 23.2 Sportsmanship and gamesmanship among sporting professionals

Figure 23.2 An act of sportsmanship

Figure 23.3 China's badminton players are disqualified from the 2012 Olympics for gamesmanship as they played to lose to give them a better draw in the next round

Key word

Deviance – behaviour that goes against the moral values or laws of the sport

Types of deviance at elite levels of sport and physical activity

Sport is said to reflect society, including examples of deviant behaviour. We think of sport as something positive for the social, physical and emotional health benefits it can bring, but is it also true that sport reflects the deviant side of society? Can you think of examples of the following deviant behaviour in sport?

- violence
- use of performance-enhancing drugs
- match fixing
- racism
- sexism

Violence in sport

Actions

Are sports supposed to be violent? Copy Table 23.3 and complete by placing a tick against the sports you consider to be violent.

Sport	Violent or non-violent 'Yes/No'
Badminton	
Gymnastics	
Football	
Archery	
American football	
Mixed martial arts	
White water rafting	
Wrestling	
Judo	
Swimming	
Rugby	
Boxing	

Table 23.3 Are some sports and physical activity naturally violent?

If violence is allowed within the sport through the rules, for example, in boxing the aim is to inflict harm on the opponent, then those that perform within the rules are clearly not being deviant as they are conforming to the rules of the activity. However, even in violent sports we still see deviant behaviour. For example, see Figure 23.4. But this type of behaviour is not just restricted to more violent sports – Luis Suarez, an international footballer, has been banned for biting opponents and he has also been accused of diving and racial abuse of other players.

Figure 23.4 Mike Tyson bit Evander Holyfield's ear during a bout in 1997. Sports Illustrated magazine ran the front page headline 'MADMAN A crazed Mike Tyson disgraces himself and his sport'

Performance-enhancing drugs

As we saw in Chapter 14, performance-enhancing drugs can artificially increase an athlete's performance, making them attractive to those who are desperate to win for the rewards winning offers, for example, fame and fortune.

Match-fixing

Due to the large sums of money involved, some sports performers are tempted to underperform in order to affect the outcome of the game. For example, Lou Vincent was offered £130,000 to underperform in four cricket matches. In football, more than 50 arrests were made in Italy as part of a football match-fixing inquiry; Delroy Facey was given a two-and-a-half-year sentence for his part in match-fixing.

Racism in sport

Actions

Research the following campaigns:
- Show Racism the Red Card
  http://www.theredcard.org
- Media Against Racism in Sport
  http://www.coe.int/t/dg4/cultureheritage/mars/default_en.asp
- Racism. It Stops With Me
  https://itstopswithme.humanrights.gov.au

Popular sports such as football are used to promote anti-racism, but despite the campaigns racism still exists in sport, between players or between players and opposition fans.

Sexism in sport

Sport was traditionally seen as something that only men participated in. Clearly this position has changed drastically but sexism still occurs in sport. According to data reported on by the BBC more than 40% of elite sportswomen in Great Britain have experienced sexism in sport (source: Women's Sport Week 2015). Sexism issues reported were unequal pay, underrepresentation in positions of power, sexist abuse, trolling in social media and sexist representation in the media.

The reasons for, and consequences of, deviance at elite level

Why do people cheat in sport?

- The external rewards on offer of
  - fame, international stardom
  - large sponsorship deals worth millions
  - place in 'higher' team to increase weekly wages.
- If a player feels like a commodity rather than part of a team.
- If the player is under pressure to perform from sport management and feels unable to do so.
- If the player is under pressure to cheat as requested by sports management, for example, the coach.
- They believe they won't get caught.
- They believe others are so why shouldn't they.

Actions

Discuss in small groups and report back to the group on your ideas of how NGBs of sport use punishment to try to prevent deviant behaviour of players. Compare your ideas with those in Table 23.4. Copy the table and add your ideas.

Punishment	How it works
Yellow card	Player is reminded to play fairly or risk removal from the game
Red card	Player is removed from the game and therefore no longer a 'threat' to other players
Sin bins	Temporary suspension to allow players to regain their composure, become more calm so that mentally they are ready to play again
Fines	Encourage people to behave appropriately as they don't wish to lose income
Bans	The threat of stopping people playing for a number of games is seen as a warning to others and also can help players change their behaviour as they don't want to miss matches

Table 23.4 Forms of punishment in sport for deviant behaviour

Sport is supposed to be about fair play, but as we have seen, there are many reasons why performers are tempted to cheat in sport. If a player is caught cheating, action is taken against them in the form of sanctions.

These sanctions are designed to dissuade them, or others from cheating again. They include:

- bad reputation
- loss of earnings through fines, bans or exclusion, for example Alex Rodriguez, (American baseball player) was banned for 162 games, and lost over $22 million in wages due to steroid use
- loss of medals or awards won while cheating (for example, returning Olympic medals)
- loss of sponsorship
- loss of opportunity to play (lifetime ban)
- imprisonment (for actions outside of the law, for example, match-fixing, GBH).

Check your understanding

4. Identify two types of deviance in sport.

5. Give two examples of sanctions or punishment NGBs can use to reduce deviant behaviour in sport.

PRACTICE QUESTIONS

1. Which one of the following is an example of sportsmanship?

   A Kicking the ball off of the field of play to delay the throw in so your team have chance to get back in position.
   B Deliberately committing a foul so that the game stops to allow a substitution.
   C Letting the referee know that you were the last person to touch the ball before it went out of bounds.
   D Clapping your opponent when they make a mistake.

2. Give an example of gamesmanship in sport.

3. Explain why national governing bodies such as the Football Association have fair play awards.

4. Explain a possible consequence for an elite performer if caught taking performance-enhancing drugs.

5. Assess whether sportsmanship has a role in today's sport and physical activity.

Study hints
Make sure you read all of the options carefully, as the beginning of option A and option D could be mistaken for sportsmanship.

Summary

- Sporting behaviour can be classified as sportsmanship or gamesmanship.
- Due to the pressures on elite performers to perform well some resort to deviant behaviour.
- Deviant behaviour in sport can result in loss of
  - earnings
  - sponsorship
  - status
  - reputation
  - medals.

Useful websites

Sportsmanship still exists sports compilation
https://www.youtube.com/watch?v=b-j-sNRHhp8

Sportsmanship
http://kidshealth.org/teen/food_fitness/sports/sportsmanship.
html#

Banned drugs found in 3,800 samples in 2014, says Wada
http://www.bbc.co.uk/sport/0/33686397

Doping cases at the Olympics, 1968-2012
http://sportsanddrugs.procon.org/view.resource.
php?resourceID=004420

Show Racism the Red Card
http://www.theredcard.org

Media Against Racism in Sport
http://www.coe.int/t/dg4/cultureheritage/mars/default_en.asp

Racism. It Stops With Me
https://itstopswithme.humanrights.gov.au

Learning goals

By the end of this chapter you should know:

- what you need to do to complete your practical assessment
- what you need to do to complete your personal exercise programme.

Your exam is made up of four parts. The first two parts are written exams and together they account for 60% of the available marks for this course. The remaining 40% is called non examined assessment or NEA and is also made of two parts, the practical and the personal exercise programme (PEP). This chapter looks at the requirements of the NEA in more detail.

Practical performance

You will be assessed in three different practical activities. Your school may allow you some choice of activity, but even if they do it must be from the approved GCSE PE activity list. Some of the approved activities

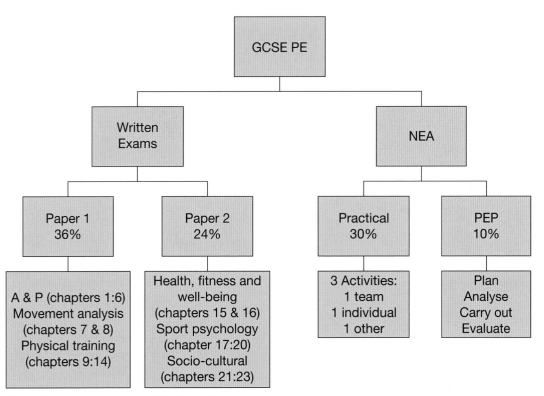

Figure 24.1 Components of the GCSE PE qualification

Figure 24.2 Squash can be played as a team or singles activity but not both

are listed below, ask your teacher if you can see the full list. The activities are divided into team and individual. A team activity is simply one that involves you playing or performing with someone else, for example, badminton doubles and dance can be team activities. You will need to select one team, one individual and a third activity, either team or individual.

EXAMPLE TEAM ACTIVITIES	EXAMPLE INDIVIDUAL ACTIVITIES	EXAMPLE *SPECIALIST TEAM ACTIVITIES	EXAMPLE *SPECIALIST INDIVIDUAL ACTIVITIES
Basketball	Boxing	Wheelchair basketball	Boccia
Hockey	Athletics	Table cricket	Polybat
Volleyball	Badminton	Powerchair football	
Badminton	Squash		
Squash	Table tennis		
Table tennis	Swimming		
Rowing	Skiing		
	Snowboarding		
	Sculling		

Table 24.1

*The specialist activities are available only to those students with a physical disability and in line with entry criteria set out by that activity's National Governing Body.

Once you have made your selection your teachers will assess your performance in these activities, giving you a mark for your ability to:

- Demonstrate skills in isolation. This is your opportunity to show how technically good you are without having to worry about opposition or being in a performance situation.
- Demonstrate skills in a competitive situation, for example, in a full game or conditioned practice.

Your teachers will be looking to see whether you:

- apply the correct techniques
- make good tactical decisions
- change tactics if not working
- are fit enough for your activity
- have the right mental approach to performance
- apply the rules
- follow safety guidelines.

Figure 24.3 Demonstrating skills in a competitive situation

A moderator will visit the school near the end of your course and ask to see selected individuals. Your teacher will inform you if you have been selected for moderation; if you have you will be asked to demonstrate your performance again so that the moderator can agree the marks given by your teacher.

Personal exercise programme

You will need to:

- plan
- perform and monitor
- evaluate

your PEP.

You will be marked on your ability to analyse your current fitness and performance in any activity from the practical list and use this analysis to create a suitable exercise programme that aims to increase your fitness in a way that will impact positively on your performance.

Figure 24.4 A PARQ contains a set of questions about your health and helps you decide if you are healthy enough to exercise

Planning Your PEP

You should have the basic knowledge required to start planning your PEP, if not re-read the chapters on physical training (chapters 9, 10, 11 and 12), as a lot of the knowledge you will need to consider is included there.

You should plan a PEP as part of your practical work. If your PEP is going to be effective in improving fitness it needs to be well thought out and continually evaluated to check you are doing the right things and that your body is adapting.

Development of a PEP should go through the following stages:

Planning

Check you can increase your activity level safely by completing a PARQ (see Chapter 10).

Identify your goals:

- What activity do you want to get fit for and why?
- What are your main weaknesses in that activity? What is really preventing you from performing better?
- Which component of fitness would help improve these weaknesses?
- Which weakness is the most critical in improving your performance?
- Find out how fit you currently are:
  - Carry out a number of different fitness tests.
  - Record your results.
- Identify your fitness strengths and weaknesses by analysing your fitness test results.
- Select the areas of fitness you need to work on based on:
  - your goals
  - current fitness weakness.
- Set and record SMART targets that relate to your main goal (see Chapter 18).
- Choose a training method to suit your goal:
  - For example, continuous training to improve cardiovascular fitness or weight training to improve strength.
  - Record your reasons for selecting this training method. Explain how it will bring about the training adaptations you want to increase fitness and the impact this will have on your performance.

Actions

Look at Figure 24.5. Can you create something similar for a weakness related to one of your activities?

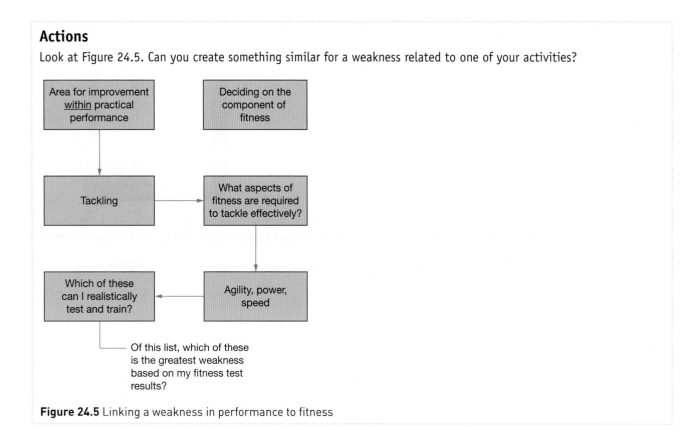

Figure 24.5 Linking a weakness in performance to fitness

- Decide on activities and workload to suit your training method that will allow you to reach your goal:
  – Number of sessions.
  – Intensity of first session.
  – The principles of training that will be applied over the course of the programme.
- Decide on the warm-up you will use and the cool-down, justifying how these will be appropriate to your exercise session.

Performing and monitoring

- Carry out your planned PEP session.
- Collect data before, during and after the session.
  – For example, heart rate values if you are working on cardiovascular endurance.
  – For example, the number of reps or sets completed if working on muscular endurance.
  – For example, the weight lifted if working on strength.
- Collect data when you play your activity between PEP sessions. Have you noticed any difference in your play? Are you more effective or just the same? It's ok not to improve but you should still try to find a way of measuring your performance in your activity.
  – For example, if a racket sport are the number of unforced errors, going down?
  – For example, if a team game, how many successful tackles made in the last 10 minutes of the game compared to the first.

- Plan any adjustments to the next PEP session and justify these in terms of the relevant principles of training.
- Re-assess the component of fitness you are hoping to improve, for example, after three PEP sessions, is there any difference? Do you need to make further adjustments to your training?
- Keep a record of everything – you will need it in your write up.

Actions

Look at Figure 24.6.
1. What aspect of fitness would the performer need to work on to bring about this target?
2. How could this target be changed to a fitness target but still bring about the required improvement in performance?
3. Think about your personal exercise programme; how can you review your targets and goals to see if they are effective?

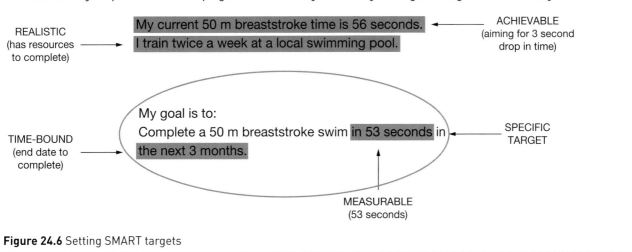

Figure 24.6 Setting SMART targets

Evaluating

Once the programme has finished it is time to evaluate it. You should:

- Repeat the fitness test that measures the component of fitness that was the focus of your PEP.
- Analyse any data you collected before, during and after completing the PEP.
- Summarise and present the analysed data.
- Evaluate the data you collected – what is it telling you?
  - Did your fitness improve?
  - Has your performance improved?
  - Were you able to increase the intensity of any of the activities you completed as part of your PEP?
- Evaluate your goal.
  - Did you achieve what you wanted to?
  - If you didn't, why not? Could you have done something different?
  - Did your body adapt to the training? If not, why not? How could you alter the programme? If it did adapt why did it?
- Make recommendations for future amendments to the PEP to continue to improve.

Figure 24.7 Choose the right method to present your data

Actions

Using your list of fitness strengths/weaknesses (based on your fitness test results):

(a) List the components of fitness you need to improve.

(b) Identify the component that has the most impact on performance.

(c) Explain the impact the weakness is having on performance and say why.

(d) Identify a training method to improve this component of fitness.

(e) Explain how you would use the principles of training to improve this component of fitness.

Summary

- You will be assessed in three different practical activities as a performer.
- You will need to complete a PEP for your assessment.
- The practical and PEP are worth 40% of your exam.

Glossary

< - this is the symbol for less than

> - this is the symbol for more than

Abduction – movement of the limb away from the body

Achievable goal – a task you know you can complete because you have the ability to do so

Adaptations – changes made to the body as a result of regular training, for example, an increase in strength is a training adaptation

Adduction – movement of the limb inwards and across the centre of the body

Aerobic – with oxygen

Aerobic activity – long duration, medium-intensity exercise, for example, playing a team game over a long period of time, for example, a 90-minute football match

Aerobic respiration – production of energy using oxygen

Aerobic training – continuous training at moderate intensity using oxygen for energy production

Alveoli – found at the end of the bronchioles, they are the sites of gaseous exchange

Anabolic steroid – synthetic hormone resembling testosterone; used to promote muscle growth

Anaerobic – without oxygen

Anaerobic activity – short duration, high-intensity exercise, for example, serving an 'ace' in tennis or running 100 m

Anaerobic respiration – production of energy without using oxygen

Anaerobic training – repeated periods of intense work followed by recovery within the training session; energy production is without oxygen during the intense periods of work

Antagonistic muscle pairs – pairs of muscles that work together to bring about movement. In order to allow the agonist to contract, the antagonist muscle relaxes

Atlas and axis – the two vertebrae at the top of the vertebral column that connect the vertebral column to the cranium

Atria – the plural of atrium, the upper chambers of the heart

Axis – something that the body, or a body part, can rotate about

Balanced diet – consuming all the different nutrients in the correct quantities

Baseline data (fitness) – initial collection of fitness test data so we can compare fitness levels before and after training

Basic skill – a simple skill requiring basic movement patterns or little decision-making to execute, for example, running

Beta blockers – presents stimulation to body systems, used to control heart rhythm

Blood pressure – pressure exerted by the blood on the walls of the blood vessel

Bronchioles – smaller branches off of the bronchi within the lungs

Bronchus – a part of the airway for the transfer of air into the lungs. There is a left and right bronchus, one for each lung. Together they are referred to as bronchi

By-product – something additional that is made during a process, for example, acid during energy production

Cardiac muscle – specialised muscle found in the heart

Circuit training – a number of different exercises at stations; rotate from one exercise to the next

Closed skill – a skill performed in a stable, unchanging environment, for example, a gymnast completing a vault

Commercialisation – making a product available for purchase

Complex skill – a skill that requires a lot of thought and concentration before it is executed, for example, playing a through ball in hockey

Components of a lever system – the parts that make up a lever system, for example, in the body this would be a bone, a joint, a muscle and the body weight

Components of fitness – these are the areas we can train to improve to make sure we are able to meet the demands for our particular activity

Concurrent feedback – information about the movement being carried out given at the same time that the skill is being performed

Concussion – temporary brain injury due to violent blow to the head or a fall

Conscious control – we need to think about the movement we want the muscles to do in order to execute it; it will not happen automatically

Continua – plural of continuum

Continuous training – working at a moderate steady pace for a minimum of 30 minutes

Continuum – a continuous line between two extremes, for example, open–closed are two extremes, a door that is 'ajar' would be indicated somewhere on the continuum between open and closed

Cranium – anatomical name for the skull

Deoxygenated blood – blood that is returning to the lungs to pick up fresh oxygen

Deviance – behaviour that goes against the moral values or laws of the sport

Deviancy – doing something against the norms or values of society

Diastolic blood pressure – blood pressure exerted on the walls of the arteries when the heart is resting, for example, between heartbeats

Dislocate – the separation of two (or more) bones where they meet at a joint

Dislocation – an injury at a joint where the bones are forced out of their normal position

Distributed practice – the repeated practice of a skill for a set amount of time with recovery periods during which the performer may rest or engage in a different task

Diuretics – a drug that reduces the amount of water in the body

Dorsi flexion – flexion of the foot in an upward direction by bringing toes up towards shin

Exercise – a form of physical activity done to maintain or improve health and/or fitness; it is not competitive sport

Expiration – breathing out

Expired air – air we breathe out of the lungs

Extension – increasing the angle between bones at a joint, for example, when straightening the arm at the elbow

Extrinsic feedback – information about the movement being carried out from external sources, for example, from a coach, in an attempt to improve performance

Fartlek training – training that involves a change in pace or intensity and varied terrains

Fast twitch or type II muscle fibres – can generate more force but tire more quickly, so are used in anaerobic work

Fitness: the ability to meet the demands of the environment

FITT – is made up of four sub-principles: frequency, intensity, time and type

Fixed practice – the repeated practice of a whole skill so that it becomes well learnt

Flexion – reducing the angle between bones at a joint, for example, when bending the arm at the elbow

Fractures – a break or crack in a bone

Frontal axis – line passing through the body horizontally from left to right

Frontal plane – line dividing the body vertically into front and back

Gamesmanship – bending the rules/laws of a sport without actually breaking them

Gaseous exchange – swapping of oxygen and carbon dioxide due to a pressure gradient

Goal – an aim or task you set yourself; something you want to achieve

Health – a state of complete emotional, physical and social well-being and not merely the absence of disease and infirmity

High-organisation skill – a skill that cannot be broken down easily into smaller parts, for example, a golf swing

Home nations – England, Scotland, Wales and Northern Ireland

Hypertrophy – an increase in size of muscle fibres

Individual differences/needs – matching training to the requirements of an individual

Insertion – the end of the muscle that is attached to the bone that will move when the muscle contracts

Inspiration – breathing in

Inspired air – air we breathe into the lungs

Interval training – a form of intermittent training where breaks are built into the training session so that the performer can recover before working again. This training method allows the performer to work at higher intensities

Intrinsic feedback – information about the movement being carried out from the performers own body that can be used to detect errors and improve performance

Involuntary muscle – muscle that is not consciously controlled by the individual, for example, the muscles in the digestive system

L/min – unit of measurement to show the volume of fluid flowing in a minute. It is used here to represent cardiac output, for example, the number of litres of blood leaving the heart per minute

Lactate – formed from lactic acid

Lactic acid – a by-product of anaerobic respiration

Lateral flexion – sideways bending movement

Leisure time – free time; time where the individual can choose to spend it how they wish, for example, not doing work or chores

Lever systems – created in the body by the musculo-skeletal system

Lifestyle choice – the choices we make about how we live and behave that impact on our health

Long-term training effect – an adaptation to the body that takes place over a long period of time due to regular training

Low-organisation skill – a skill that can be broken down easily into smaller parts, for example, phases of the high jump

Lumen – the space inside a tube, for example, the space the blood flows through inside the blood vessel

Macronutrient – nutrients that are required in large quantities in our diet: carbohydrates, fats and protein

Manual guidance – the performer is physically moved by the coach into the correct position to perform a technique to provide information about the feel of the movement

Massed practice – the repeated practice of a skill over a period of time without a break for recovery

Measureable goal – provides a way of checking to see if you have improved

Mechanical guidance – the coach uses an aid to move the performer into the correct position when learning a skill, for example, a tumbling belt in gymnastics

Mental rehearsal – forming a mental picture of a skill or technique you are about to perform

Micronutrient – nutrients that are required in small quantities in our diet: vitamins and minerals

Mitochondria – found in the muscles, they are the site of aerobic respiration

Muscle fatigue – drop in ability of the muscle to carry out physical work due to lack of energy

Muscle fibre types – can be fast or slow twitch. Slow twitch fibres are good for endurance activities; they are slow to tire but not powerful. Fast twitch fibres can generate more force but tire more quickly

Narcotic analgesics – drugs used to suppress pain

Normative data tables – a table of other people's scores on a fitness test that we can use to judge our fitness levels against

Open skill – a skill performed in a changing environment where the performer must react and adapt due to the actions of others, for example, a tackle in rugby

Optimum weight – the weight someone should be based on their sex, height, bone structure and muscle girth

Origin – the fixed end of the muscle attachment; when the muscle contracts this end of the bone will not move

Origin and insertion – the points where a muscle attaches to a bone

Osteoporosis – health condition where the bones of the skeleton become brittle and more likely to break

Overtraining – a decrease in performance due to insufficient rest and recovery from training sessions

Oxygen debt – the shortfall of oxygen during exercise that must be 'repaid' during recovery

Oxygenated blood – blood that is travelling to the body carrying oxygen for use by the muscles

PARQ – physical activity readiness questionnaire. A series of questions that should be asked before engaging in increased levels of physical activity to ensure there are not health issues that should be taken into account when planning intensity of exercise

Passive smoking – breathing in the harmful effects of someone else's smoke

PEP – personal exercise programme. You will need to plan, analyse and evaluate a PEP as part of your assessment

Peptide hormones – protein hormones naturally occurring in the body

Performance – how well a task is completed

Performance-enhancing drugs (PEDs) – supplements taken by an athlete so that they can perform better due to additional or enhanced training adaptations brought about by the drug

Plane – an imaginary line or flat surface that is used to divide the body

Plantar flexion – extension of the ankle through pointing of the toes

Platelets – blood cells that clot together to heal a wound in the skin

Plyometric training – a form of intermittent training that develops power and strength

Principles of training – a set of ideas/values that should be followed in order to make training effective

Progressive overload – to gradually increase the amount of work done so that fitness gains occur, but without potential for injury

Realistic goal – a task you can complete because you have the resources to do so

Resistance training – a training method where the performer has to manage an additional weight or resistance when carrying out the exercise; used to increase strength, power or speed

Reversibility – the loss of training adaptations due to a reduction in training levels

Rotation – circular movement

Sagittal axis – line passing through the body horizontally from front to back

Sagittal plane – line dividing the body vertically into left and right sides

Sedentary lifestyle – a lifestyle where the individual has limited or no physical activity

Short-term effects – something that doesn't last for very long, for example, being out of breath after running, but after a few minutes breathing returns to normal

Site of aerobic respiration – place in the muscles where oxygen is used to produce energy

Skeletal muscle – muscles attached to the skeleton that contract to bring about movement

Sledging – a term used in cricket when players try to gain an advantage by insulting the opposition

Slow twitch or type I muscle fibres – good for endurance activities as they are slow to tire

SMART targets – specific, measureable, achievable, realistic, time-bound

Socio-economic group – a way of classifying people by their occupation. For example, managerial or lower supervisory

Soft tissue – any part of the body that is not made up of bone

Specific goal – a clear, focused goal

Specificity – matching training to the requirements of an activity or a position within an activity

Sponsorship – cash or resources paid for a commercial return through increased exposure of a brand

Sport England – independent government organisation responsible for developing sport in England

Sports injury – injuries that arise from taking part in sport or physical activity

Sportsmanship – qualities of fairness, following the rules, being gracious in defeat or victory

Stereotypes – these are commonly held, oversimplified, preconceived ideas about a person or group. They can be positive or negative

Stimulants – something that raises the nervous activity of the body

Systolic blood pressure – blood pressure when the heart is contracting

Taper – reducing the amount of something, in training this means reducing intensity of training prior to competition

Terminal feedback – information given about a movement after it has been carried out

Test protocol – method used to carry out the fitness test

Tidal volume – is the movement of air into or out of the lungs in one normal breath

Time-bound – a deadline to complete the task by

Training thresholds – the upper and lower limits of target zones. Target zones are the heart rate ranges an individual should work within to achieve aerobic or anaerobic gains

Transverse plane – line dividing the body horizontally from front to back

Variable practice – a mixture of massed and distributed practice within a coaching session to allow changes of tasks so that the same skill can be repeated in different situations

Vascular shunting – increase in blood flow to active areas during exercise by diverting blood away from inactive areas

Vasoconstriction – mechanism to reduce blood flow by reducing internal diameter of a blood vessel

Vasodilation – mechanism to increase blood flow by widening the internal diameter of a blood vessel

Verbal guidance – this is the use of a verbal explanation from the coach to the performer about the correct way to complete a technique

Vertebrae – bones that form the spine or vertebral column

Vertiebral column – forms the spine in the body. It is made up of a number of vertebrae

Vertical axis – line passing through the body vertically from top to bottom

Visual guidance – the use of a demonstration (or similar) to provide information to the performer to aid their learning of a skill

Vital capacity – is the maximum amount of air that can be expired after a maximal inspiration

Voluntary muscle – muscle that is consciously controlled by the individual, for example, the muscles of the skeletal system

WADA – World Anti-Doping Agency

Weight training – is a form of resistance training carried out to improve strength or muscular endurance

Index